British Women Novelists and the Review Periodical

ANALYTICAL
BRITISH CRITIC.
CRITICAL REVIEW.
MONTHLY REVIEW.

British Women Novelists *and* *the* Review Periodical

MEGAN PEISER

Johns Hopkins University Press

Baltimore

© 2026 Johns Hopkins University Press
First printed in the United States of America on acid-free paper
2 4 6 8 9 7 5 3 1

Johns Hopkins University Press
2715 North Charles Street
Baltimore, Maryland 21218
www.press.jhu.edu

Library of Congress Cataloging-in-Publication Data is available.
ISBN 978-1-4214-5407-8 (paperback)
ISBN 978-1-4214-5408-5 (ebook)

A catalog record for this book is available from the British Library.

*Special discounts are available for bulk purchases of this book. For more information,
please contact Special Sales at specialsales@jh.edu.*

EU GPSR Authorized Representative
LOGOS EUROPE, 9 rue Nicolas Poussin, 17000, La Rochelle, France
E-mail: Contact@logoseurope.eu

CONTENTS

I have written this book from the traditional and ancestral lands of the Anishinaabe people, specifically the Three Fires Confederacy comprised of the Ojibwe, Odawa, and Potawatomi. Waawiyatanong, or the place currently called Detroit, has held me while I worked, and I am grateful for how this land fed me and made my life possible for the past several years. I also wrote and conducted research for this book on the traditional lands of the Peoria, Osage, Ogalala Sioux, and Kickapoo. I have presented research from this book on lands all across Turtle Island and am deeply indebted to the original stewards of these lands for holding them in health so that I could live and work, even briefly, upon them. As a citizen of Choctaw Nation of Oklahoma, I acknowledge my tribal removal homelands in Oklahoma and our ancestral homelands at Nanih Waiya, in the place currently called Mississippi, for carrying the seven generations before me and many ancestors more into life so that I could be here to write these words.

The writing of this monograph would not have been possible without the help and input of many. This list will be wholly incomplete, and I hope that any who find themselves among the silences here will know that my heart speaks loudly to them in gratitude. I must acknowledge the Reviews themselves, followed closely by their guardians. The research for this book would not have been at all possible without the archives gathered in the University of Missouri Special Collections, the microfilm and historical periodicals especially. Thanks to librarians Kelli Hansen, Anne Barker, Dominique Daniels, and Emily Spunaugle for all of your support in this research and access to materials. Thank you to the staff at the Valence House Museum, especially Karen Rushton.

My gratitude to mentors who believed in this work when it was a twinkle of an idea and encouraged my scholarship in every way: Devoney Looser, Stephen Karian, George Justice, Michael Yonan, Margaret Ezell, Sean Grass, Ann Hawkins, Jennifer Snead, and Marta Kvande.

Thank you to the folks who read various pieces of this work in draft, outline, spreadsheet, and every messy form and who encouraged me to continue doing this work even when I was still figuring out what it was. To Betty Schellenberg, Michelle Levy, and the entire Women's Book History crew—my work is richer and more robust for the time I spent with you and the knowledge that you shared with me. I am grateful to those who have talked with me over these ideas and shared in my devotion to periodicals—Jennie Batchelor, Manushag Powell, Rachel King, Hannah Dougherty Hudson, and Elizabeth Neiman. Thank you to Emily Friedman for always making space for my voice and for work in our fields even as we were still making it up and to Ben Pauley for living the work of book history and digital humanities with joy, passion, and realness. Thank you to Jenni Spitulnik for keeping me upright when I thought I couldn't keep going and for sitting with me for the earliest writing of most of these pages. This book would literally not have come to being without your presence, your support, and your love. Thank you to James Ascher for so much bibliography chatter. Thank you to Laura Mandell and Anthony Mandel for your support, advice, and scholarship. Thank you to Kirstyn Leuner for showing me I could be my own rock.

Our ideas require space, community, discourse, nourishment, and care to grow. I could not have grown any of these ideas without places for them to live and develop. I am indebted to the many communities that have folded me into their arms. To the Titas writing group and the SpaceCats Discord server—you made virtual writing groups and online writing support a real and active help for me as I molded this work into what it has become. Thank you to the American Society for Eighteenth-Century Studies (ASECS), especially the Women's Caucus, for giving me a home, a community, and a place to share my work. Thank you to the Aphra Behn Society for blazing a pathway for feminist scholarship on women writers and bringing so many of these scholars together. A special nod to the 18th/19th Century Group folks from Mizzou, especially Ruth Knezevich, Noah Herringman, Lily Gurten-Wachter, Miranda Mattingly, Allison Rutledge, Sean Franzel, Elizabeth Chang, and Heather Heckman-Mckenna. Thank you to Eugenia Zuroski, who was the first to welcome all of me into the field of eighteenth-century studies. Thank you to the intertribal community of Metro Detroit, my brothers and sisters and relatives beyond the binary who remind me every day of my sacredness and the importance of my life and work here in this time and place. Thank you to my ASECS cohort: Cassie Childs, Jessica Cook, Leah Orr, Sarah Creel, and Amanda Springs.

This research was also made possible by the financial support of several grants and fellowships. I extend my thanks to the Institute for Citizens and Scholars

WW Fellowship in Women's Studies, the Chawton House Library visiting fellows program, the Bibliographical Society of America (BSA) and ASECS research grants, the BSA New Scholars program, the BSA William L. Mitchell prize, the ASECS Women's Caucus Editing and Translation Prize, and Oakland University's faculty research fellowship. Thank you to the Wellcome Library for being a feminist place where I could work and dream and for making databases accessible, without which I could not have obtained multiple copies of many of the periodicals that I used for this research. Thank you to Gillian Dow and all of the staff from my time at Chawton House Library and to my fellow fellows: Lindsey Eckert, Hellen Williams, and Aran Ruth. That space and you folks made my writing feel alive. Thank you to Kirsten Saxton, Jason Faar, and Emily Spunaugle for taking pictures for me at far-flung libraries and to all of the librarians who sent me quick snapshots, especially during the COVID-19 pandemic, when travel was impossible. Thank you to Chelsea Phillips for your genealogy help. Thank you, Richard Roberts, for help with reading the Fanshawe wills. Thank you, Deirdre Marculescu, for sharing so much about the Fanshawes with me.

Thank you to Kate Ozment for reading my writing, for your encouragement, for the excitement of discoveries, for helping me say "no" to things so I could make time for this book, for the camaraderie, for the support in taking a different path than the one you intended. Thank you for roaring the roar of feminist book history. Thank you for dog and tattoo pictures, thank you for the cheerleading. Thank you for being in the trenches with me. Thank you to Emily Spunaugle for the tea, the tea, the tea, the travel, the idea sharing, the archives hopping, the draft reading, the library support at every turn, the sentence smoothing, the tracking down of things that I *know* should exist. Thank you for splitting meals in London, sheltering in place, fighting and making up, long walks, 'post hauling, and all the garden work that kept me sane. I don't have enough words for you, but I will never sip tea out of my great-great-aunt's china without holding you in my heart.

Thank you to all of my family, who never flinched at the person I am: writing and reading and scribbling and ideas. Thank you to my parents for celebrating my desire to read, to my beloved great-aunt Kaye for believing in me as a writer, and to my brother, Thorin, for your unfailing faith in me as a human and the assurance in life you gave me by always being by my side. Thank you to Matt, and Cameron, and Charlotte for being the place I go home to. And thank you to the dachshunds, past and present, whose companionship I relied on to write these pages: Rory, Burney, and Jasper. Coqueli, too.

Introduction

> The extensive plan of your critical observations,—which, not confined to works of utility or ingenuity, is equally open to those of frivolous amusement, and yet worse than frivolous dullness,— encourages me to seek for your protection, since,—perhaps for my sins!—it entitles me to your annotations.[1]

> The reviews, however, as they have not made, will not, I trust, mar me. "Evelina" made its way all by itself; it was well spoken of, indeed, in all the reviews, compared with general novels, but it was undistinguished by any quotation, and only put in the Monthly Catalogue, and only allowed a short single paragraph.[2]

Addressing her debut novel, *Evelina*, "To the Authors of the Monthly and Critical Reviews," Frances Burney exhibited a keen familiarity with the influence and power that these two periodicals exerted over the English reading public. The woman who would become one of the most popular novelists of the eighteenth century names her deferential plea the "natural inheritance, and constant resource, from time immemorial, of the Dedicator," drawing attention to the "annotations" she expects (or rather, is "entitl[ed]" to) in the book reviews of her work. She calls these book reviews (above) an "extensive plan" of "critical observations." Though Burney was a first-time author, her familiarity with the English book market and its Reviewing[3] organ, the twin lungs of the *Monthly Review* and the *Critical Review*, highlights the degree to which eighteenth-century readers and authors acknowledged book reviewing as a known and central system by which publications were cast into the hands, minds, and memories of readers.

Twenty years later, the seasoned author writes privately in response to her father, Charles Burney's, outrage at the *Monthly Review*'s criticisms of her third novel, *Camilla*. Burney herself is up in arms, claiming that "Works of this kind [novels] are judged by the many: works of science, History and philosophy and voyages and travels, and poetry frequently owe their fate to the sentiments of the first Critics who brand or extol them."[4] She goes on to declare that novels "may be aided, or injured by criticism; but it will not stop their being read, though it may prejudice their readers. They want no Recommendation for being handed about other than being new, and they frequently become established, or sink into oblivion, before the high Literary Tribunal has brought them to Trial." In this letter, Burney casts about for reasons to ignore the Reviews, noting that *Evelina* "made it" without superfluous praise, though it was noticed by the critics. Only a week later, however, Burney again writes to her father "upon a second reading of the *Monthly Review*." She is willing to "confess the case to the criticisms" and calls the critiques "stronger and more important, upon re-perusal, than I had imagined, in the panic of a first survey."[5]

These three instances show Burney positioning herself as an author in relation to eighteenth-century book reviews and tracking the centrality of their publication to both immediate and long-term conceptions of the novel and each individual novel's place in the English book market. But Burney did what a modern scholar cannot: she read and understood book reviews as part of a literary system, not as singular articles related only to herself. She could see reviews as a web of other context—publishers, politics, authorial experience, genre trends, and more. The form of the Reviews as readers interacted with them, their function in a circulating system of information about literary criticism, and their purpose to guide and inform readers are all interconnected and cannot be effectively understood separately. They are not flat or static reactions *to* novels. Rather, the Reviews are dynamic and stratified vehicles for not only novel criticism but for interaction with novels by a multitude of readers (even readers who did not read the novels themselves), a forum for novelist interaction with criticism and the readerly marketplace, a teeter-totter of how to navigate what was "good" in a politicized climate, and a rocky barometer for the fluctuating boundaries of the genre. But how do modern scholars explore that system of reviews that Burney knew and understood so well when our access to periodicals is scattered and varied amid expensive paywalled databases, poorly preserved microfilm, and few hard copies? How do we make sense of what readers and writers like Burney found in Review pages that enriched their experience of the novel? And how do we incorporate that into our own understanding of the English novel today?

Review Periodicals and the English Novel

The Reviews' criticisms of literature squawked loudly into the ears of eighteenth-century and Romantic readers and writers.[6] The *Monthly Review* (1749–1845) and the *Critical Review* (1756–1817), rival periodicals, emerged as authoritative judges of literary merit and circulated their criticisms around England and beyond. The *Monthly* and the *Critical*'s stinging reviews, of novels especially, set the stage for what would become a reviewing tradition of harsh criticism against that growing genre. This tradition depended on the craze for reviewing that grew as the eighteenth century progressed. By the end of the century, the *Monthly* and the *Critical* were joined by the *Analytical Review* (1788–1798), the *Edinburgh Review* (1802–1929), and the *Quarterly Review* (1809–1967).[7] As the first established and longest running by the end of the eighteenth century, the *Monthly* and the *Critical* remained foremost sources for literature review and were together simply referred to as "the Reviews," though this name evolved to include other periodicals generally performing the same singular function.[8] Contemporaries and modern scholars alike have wondered to what degree the reviews were "puffed" or written with ulterior motives of promoting certain authors' or publishers' works, but Antonia Forster argues that the interconnected nature of the book trade in the eighteenth century meant that every periodical had some connection to a bookseller, printer, publisher, or editor who had something to gain by its success. Therefore, Ralph Griffiths (the *Monthly*) and Tobias Smollett (the *Critical*) were no different in their stakeholder editorships of the Reviews, and neither were their reviewers.[9]

Using the Review periodical as a unique and exceptional tool with which we might study the history of the English novel was first considered seriously by Joseph F. Bartolomeo in *A New Species of Criticism* (1994). His study provides extensive quoted passages from the periodicals and synthesizes the generality of their complaints, criticisms, and (occasional) praises of the genre, tying them to novelists' own anxieties about reception.[10] This earlier incorporation of book reviews to study the English novel was largely done by a cherry-picking method in which only the review of an individual novel was extracted, thereby removing it from the context of reviewing practices in general. Laura Runge brought gender to the forefront of scholarship on Review criticism of novels, insisting that we cannot evaluate the two genres together without significant attention to the masculine authorship of one and the dominantly feminine authorship of the other.[11] Runge's explication of gendered review criticism is striking, especially considering, as Laura Mandell argues, that the "construction of gender took place at the very same moment, and using the very same literary devices, as the moment and methods through which novelistic genres were formed."[12]

Scholarship on gendered authorship of novels in the late century now invariably notices the gendered criticisms the Reviews slung at it. Rachel Scarborough King and Pam Perkins have since counted reviews in their study of the gendered authorship and reception of novels and canon formation.[13] And Michael Gamer has noted that given general anxiety about prose fiction and its relationship to gender (of readers, writers, and characters) across the century, we should not be surprised that these two genres—the novel and the Review—emerged together. Gamer's tables illustrate both the increasing number of new novels published and at what rate they are reviewed, showing that "reviewers, in spite of their constant complaints about the increase of novels, maintained a fairly vigilant level of surveillance [of the genre]." Gamer's data shows an invaluable comparison, though it nonetheless leaves us asking *which* novels specifically he is talking about, as modern publishers will usually not print the extensive lists scholars collate for economy of space.[14] The problem with the established necessity of incorporating this scale of evidence from Reviews, often using quantitative methodologies, into our scholarship on the history of criticism, the English novel, and its gendered authorship is twofold: access and context. These two issues dog almost all studies of book reviews from the eighteenth century and emphasize what Burney had that we do not. And for Burney specifically, who was publishing during a unique period in women's literary history, our lack of access and context keeps us from glimpsing the influence that the system of book reviewing had on individual writers or the genre as a whole.

Burney's aforementioned interaction with book reviews comes just as women were dominating the novel-writing scene in Britain. Peter Garside, James Raven, and Rainer Schöwerling's publication data shows us that from 1790 to 1820, more novels were published by women writers than by their male counterparts—unlike any sustained period before or after (Table I.1 and Fig. I.1).[15] The Reviews confirm their data: Articles about novels by women abounded, and the gendered criticism they received flavored the literary marketplace these women were writing themselves into, which is why this book attends to this 30-year period.[16] Women had always published novels, and the proliferation of these women's works are well known contemporarily and in scholarship today. There can be no doubt of the importance and influence of women novelists from 1790

TABLE I.1
Number of New Novels Published
From Garside and Raven

	Female Author	Male Author	Authorship Still Unknown
1770s	45 *(14%)*	94 *(30%)*	174 *(56%)*
1780s	118 *(48%)*	99 *(40%)*	29 *(12%)*
1790s	260 *(38%)*	215 *(32%)*	205 *(30%)*
1800s	362 *(47%)*	289 *(38%)*	119 *(15%)*
1810s	344 *(52%)*	191 *(29%)*	127 *(19%)*
1820s	273 *(33%)*	419 *(51%)*	132 *(16%)*

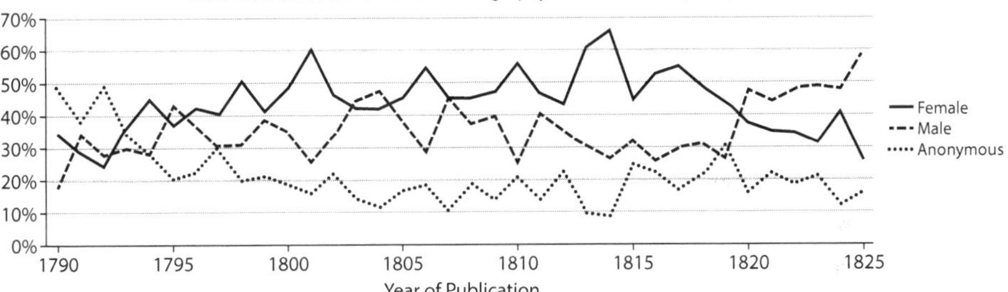

Figure I.1. Percent of New Novels by Author's Gender, 1790–1825. Taken from *The English Novel 1770–1829: A Bibliographical Survey of Prose Fiction Published in the British Isles* (2000), vols. 1 & 2.

to 1820. This period in women's literary history in particular, which Hannah Doherty Hudson calls the Minerva Press Era, benefitted from the infusion of novels by women William Lane solicited for his publishing house and circulating libraries under that goddess's name.[17] Elizabeth Neiman illustrates that Minerva Press authors tip the period's publication scale from a 233-to-231 women-to-men novel authorship ratio before Lane's press enters the scene to 345 to 286 afterward.[18] Large-scale studies of this particular moment in time are essential. Neiman argues that "different maps [of a period or topic] can help us see a territory differently, even without erasing lines already drawn with good reason."[19]

Her new map traces how Minerva Press novelists' constant borrowing of one another's textual material serves to "collectively recirculate, engage and modify commonplaces about women's nature, the social order, and . . . Romantic redefinitions of authorship and literature" out into the world, acknowledging that "no one single novel transforms the conversation."[20]

The Reviews are, as we see in the forthcoming chapters, another circulating force—sometimes propelling novelists' ideas (or criticism about them) out further, sometimes distorting authorial messages along the way. Hudson establishes the Reviews' contributions to the period's perception of novels as defined by excess. She points to the Reviews' need to categorize most novels as trash and focus on the few that rise above as a form of management of the sheer volume of output at that time. Further, these classifications serve as a catalyst, jump-starting shifts in the content and aesthetics in the novels themselves. Review perceptions, Hudson argues, "had both wide distribution and staying power. If anyone is responsible for the age's perceptions of excess, then, reviewers are certainly among the guiltiest parties."[21] What Neiman and Hudson also illustrate is scholars' growing attention to, care of, and respect for making visible the tangled web of the book market that Romantic women writers entered and shaped—and the Reviews are part of that web. The relationship between novels and reviews is one of continual interdependence, and, as George Justice notes, "paraliterary discourses, reviews and book advertisements both depend upon and enable the emergence of the literary culture that they represent as commodities."[22]

Despite this growing realm of scholarship, however, thus far most of the aforementioned studies of Romantic novel, women writer, and review relationships have depended on piecemeal studies. It has heretofore not been feasible to undertake a sustained bibliographical look at the Reviews as part of our understanding of women's dominant authorship of the English novel just as it was solidified as a respected literary genre. And while we arguably no longer live in the midst of what Clifford Siskin called the "Great Forgetting," whereby women writers from the eighteenth century and Romantic period were systemically removed from popular historical consciousness, we are still operating in an intellectual landscape that cannot access the fullness of their stratified literary marketplace because the ability to include and incorporate the fabric of the Reviews has been unavailable to us by our fractured reading of these periodical texts.

By fractured reading here, I mean that the greater circulating of ideas that the Reviews created and perpetuated through English consciousness is inaccessible to modern scholars because of our limited understanding of how the Reviews were read by contemporaries. Dipping into individual review articles as needed has left us with a collapsed conception of what book reviewing did or could do for an emerging genre like the novel. This book aims to rectify this significant oversight in our scholarship on British women novelists at the height of their dominance, the literary book market into which their productions were cast, and the form and function of book reviewing as a not yet fully acknowledged literary system. Herein I argue for the centrality of a *system* of book reviewing in the Romantic period to the buying, selling, reading, and writing of or about novels and that system's integral role in establishing and circulating popular assessments of the English novel and its feminine authorship. Using methods drawn from the intersecting fields of bibliography, book history, scholarly editing, feminist literary criticism, and digital humanities, I argue that modern scholars' lack of access to the system of eighteenth-century book reviewing has served to perpetuate gendered rhetoric about the English novel and definitions of that genre, which in turn has obscured to us, even in quantitative study, the contributions of key authors, conversations, and subgenres to the novel's development. I also provide the tool to facilitate, for the first time, scholars' access to this system: *the Novels Reviewed Database, 1790–1820* (*NRD*).

The creation of a tool to access the system of book reviewing from the late eighteenth century and Romantic period is central to the arguments that follow throughout this book. "To study eighteenth-century periodicals and to do feminist scholarly work in the eighteenth century are inseparable tasks," Jennie Batchelor and Manushag N. Powell argue at the onset of their groundbreaking volume, *Women's Periodicals and Print Culture in Britain, 1690–1820s*, and I wholeheartedly agree.[23] Periodicals like the Reviews were among the most highly circulated mediums through which women writers' works were disseminated. And while scholars have long read book reviews of Romantic novels, cited them with glee for their snarky criticisms, and pointed to their especially gendered remarks, a piecemeal approach to reading or citing Reviews is often all that is available to us because of the difficulty of accessing these periodicals or understanding them as part of a larger system. Since Bartolomeo, there has been no sustained study of the Reviews, and that is largely due to the type of bibliographical labor such a study requires.

Kate Ozment establishes in her rationale for feminist bibliography that the compiling of lists and bibliographies and the gathering together of dispersed data are themselves forms of activist bibliographical labor. This kind of labor, however, has historically been ignored in the field of book history and bibliography because of the gendered nature of this work, which is often undertaken by the feminized professional librarians, cataloguers, collectors, and curators.[24] Creating enumerative bibliographies is the root of all fields of intellectual study and especially of diversifying any field by illustrating the necessity for acknowledging and making space for missing or marginalized voices. This book, for example, would not exist without the research that Garside, Raven, and Schöwerling's capacious bibliography, *The English Novel, 1770–1829*, brought to bear on that genre's history across the period. Showing that books, writers, and voices *existed* through bibliographies provides a starting point for future study and an argument for the existence and value of these past works. Herein I use the *NRD* to make these arguments about women novelists and the Reviewing system that surrounded them.

The Reviews are stratified bibliographies of published literature in England and indices of review criticism within a complex web of relationships to people and texts. This dynamic layering of relationships is part of what makes the Reviews, and any periodical, difficult to study. Batchelor, in her focused and rich work, *The Lady's Magazine and the Making of Literary History*, debunks eighteenth-century and modern scholarly assertions about magazines and periodicals generally on account of their purpose and readers.[25] Batchelor's work upends the notion that one can only be a reader or a writer, a contributor or a critic, and instead traces a constellation of relationships between texts, readers, editors, critics, and the periodical itself. The "miscellany as method" argument she proposes forces us to reconsider contextual relationships across articles within periodicals and periodicals' relationships with texts and readers across time.[26] The periodical (or magazine), she argues, "is not a static repository of different types of content, but a dynamic, multi- and inter-mediated network in which meaning is generated by interaction, remediation, and juxtaposition."[27]

Batchelor's assertions are essential to our ability to access the Reviews as a rich cosmology of information and relationships. In the Reviews, each publication is evaluated based on a seemingly agreed-upon metric defined by the voices of the evaluators—the literary critics. Largely educated, male, and themselves invested in the book trade, the reviewers often worked to maintain a status quo of elitism in literary taste. Many of these reviewers were also literary authors themselves. Burney, her father and brothers, and indeed English novel writers, critics, readers, and fans across the long eighteenth century could and did regularly pick up a monthly issue of a book review periodical, flip its pages, and peruse critical reviews. Inside, they would find critiques of recently published works of all genres, placing them in the context of Britain's wider literary output. By skimming through Review pages to find a trove of articles devoted to a genre or topic, readers of the Reviews tapped into a literary system circulating in print—an interconnected network of voices and ideas with a set of procedures and a framework for evaluation and dissemination.

Reviews perpetuated the need for their own system: There was high and low literature, and the book-reviewing critics were needed to help differentiate between the two.[28] Each monthly issue, claiming to be a set of consensus critiques, was sent to individual subscribers, libraries, bookshops, coffeehouses, and pump rooms across the country. As they arrived, the system began its viruslike work, attaching its rhetoric and criticism to the reading minds of England, instructing them how to evaluate literature of varying genres—what to value, what to scoff at, and, in the end, what to read and/or buy. The flurry of reader reactions, real or imaginary, fed back into this system, and the Reviews acknowledged readers' opinions or faults in following issues, through both combative letters to the editor and references to readers in subsequent reviews of similar works. These monthly issues were then bound together by their subscribers, a full index to the volume provided with the December issue, and placed on the shelf as records of that year's publications. Bound volumes of the Reviews were used repeatedly as references by readers, solidifying their framework for assessing literature in the collective knowledge of the reading public.

A History of Bibliographical Studies of the English Novel

Scholars have attempted to access or reproduce the many moving pieces of England's historical book market and its relationship to novels and periodicals through methods that recreate the volume of print that the eighteenth century and Romantic period produced.[29] Quantitative studies in literary analysis have abounded since the early 2000s work by Stanford Literary Lab scholars, but as Katherine Bode notes, and we later see, quantitative studies often lack the rigor of bibliography in terms of assessment of its underlying data. In this monograph, the data are book reviews or books themselves, which aligns with work that has centered book history and bibliography in literary studies since the nineteenth century.[30] It is no surprise, then, that bibliographies, indices, and catalogues, all quantitative lists of the English novel, have been a central tool for studying that genre since before Ian Watt pushed it into the scholarly limelight in 1957 and have grown since Nancy Armstrong emphasized how these novels are integrally tied to how women understood themselves and can be understood by scholars in context to their social histories.[31]

The first of such studies, Andrew Block's *English Novel 1740–1850: A Catalogue* (1939), sold out its first print run entirely; a second edition appeared in

1961. Scholars were hungry for a complete bibliography of the English novel. Block was, until Garside, Raven, and Shöwerling's two-volume bibliography (2000), the standard reference for the genre. But Block's citations are erratic and incomplete. The introduction to Block's revised edition by John Crow highlights how the English novel, especially as written by women, would be treated over the next 30 years. Crow laments "the dismal swampy plain of the innumerable military novels, naval novels, Irish novels, dirty novels, horrid novels of the Block list" from which the "mighty mountains" of our canonical novelists rose. Slinging a particularly eighteenth-century slander, Crow accusingly asserts that the Reviews were the "nastiest of all" and calls them "Grub-street fictional journalism that wore the mask of piety." During the time when women writers reigned, he declares that "the great bulk of published fiction was the utterest trash." Crow's assertion after this mudslinging foreshadows our use of bibliographies in quantitative studies: "Block's list, rightly looked at, gives us the *data* for a chapter in the history of taste."[32] And indeed from Block, many checklists of novels and sources for data and a corpus for study grew.

W. H. McBurney filled the gap before Block's catalogue began with *A Check List of English Prose Fiction, 1700–1739* (1960), and Dorothy Blakey gave us the first list of novels largely authored by women in *The Minerva Press 1790–1820* (1939).[33] Enumerative studies of the early English novel continue and are improved upon today by Marta Kvande's *Restoration Printed Fiction: A Comprehensive and Searchable Database of Fiction Printed 1660–1700* and Leah Orr's *Novel Ventures: Fiction and Print Culture in England 1690–1730* (2017).[34] There are also the more specific, like Anne Stevens's study of the historical novel "before Scott," which considers bibliographical studies of the novel in one of its most popular subgenres.[35]

Many of these bibliographies of the English novel use book reviews to source titles of texts for which there is no currently known extant copy. We should not be surprised, then, that following the heels of English novel bibliographies, scholars would turn to enumerating book reviews. Though William Smith Ward's 1972 *Literary Reviews in British Periodicals, 1798–1820* began the work of compiling a bibliography of book review articles from the Romantic period and was followed by Donald H. Reiman's *The Romantics Reviewed* that year, it is Forster's two-volume *Index to Book Reviews in England, 1749–1800* (1990; 1997) that first took up this project for the eighteenth century.[36] Her indices remain the foremost reference source on eighteenth-century book-reviewing practices and are meticulous and accessible. Her introductions to both volumes outline the intentions of the editors of the *Monthly* and the *Critical Review* and the ways the two periodicals molded the traditions that other English periodicals would adopt. Though not an enumerative study, Derek Roper's *Reviewing before the Edinburgh* (1978) set out an essential narrative about reviewing practices in eighteenth-century England, overturning previous scholars' assertions that the Reviews were authored by hacks and were mere bullhorns to spread publishers' marketing schemes undertaken to increase sales.[37] Roper and Forster's work, along with Ward's ever-expanding indices (he also produced *British Periodicals and Newspapers 1789–1832* in 1973), piled into university libraries and brought eighteenth-century and Romantic book reviews back into scholarly research—resurrecting them from the grave of "propaganda" where they had previously been buried. These indices, though, did not put book reviews or novels into the hands of every scholar. Access remained a constant obstacle. But access is not the only obstacle, and it is not merely that we reincorporate book reviews back into our scholarship on women novelists that is so pressing; it is that we do so through a means that illuminates how the system of book reviewing contributed not only to this moment in history when women published more novels than men but also to the ways that the Reviews have shaped our own scholarly criticisms of novelists and the novel today.

A Scholarly Edition of a Literary System

The use of the aforementioned bibliographies as datasets to conduct large-scale quantitative studies of English literature has, in the last 20 years, provided invaluable insights into the book market of the period and benefitted research on women writers. In addition to addressing the problem of access, however, any study of Review periodicals must also consider their context. Katherine Bode provides a solution to the context question, addressing especially the patrons of macroanalysis and distant reading. She calls it a scholarly edition of a literary system, and that is what I have created in the *NRD* for the system of reviewing English novels in the Romantic period. Bode argues that the "lack of a scholarly object capable of representing literary-historical systems . . . is the real reason it has proved so difficult, in practice if not in theory, to integrate data-rich and traditional methods for literary-historical investigation."[38]

Even when *access* is not the central issue for scholars who have data to work with, Bode asserts that the aforementioned methods of data analysis do not have the means to consider the context of that data to begin with. "Distant reading and macroanalysis," she notes, "take the core object and premise of the New Criticism—the decontextualized text as the source of all meaning—to a conclusion rendered more abstract and extreme by the manner of texts under consideration" and, in the process, strip out essential contextual markers and nuance.[39] What is lost sits in that gap between the context of the texts under study and the conclusions drawn by distant reading. This is to our detriment, because when we are unaware of this gap, we perpetuate misconceptions and problematic conclusions in our reuse of such data. In our devotion to studying the English novel, we incorporate data from Garside, Raven, and Shöwerling, or McBurney, or Stevens without minding the gap of assumptions, absences, and constraints on that data: e.g., these publication dates are for first editions only; anonymous authorship is not always about shame; English translators of foreign novels are not listed as authors; and women in particular are writing in subgenres we are disregarding in our data.

Distant reading as a "new" concept also overlooks that bibliographers have been working with datasets for ages. Bringing together multiple versions of a single printed work or tracking changes over time is the work of bibliography, but the counting and tracking are deeply connected to context. Bode proposes an alternative to thinking of distant reading and bibliography as at odds with nuanced literary criticism: "Not close or distant reading, or a simple integration of the two, but a new scholarly object of representing literary works in their historical context, one capable of managing the documentary records complexity."[40] Like the familiar scholarly editions of individual primary works that are central to literary studies, a scholarly edition of a literary system is much the same: It provides a curated text with extensive contextual materials accessible to scholars and built to guide them in their use of the edition. It has a note on the text outlining exactly what that text is, what decisions were made in its curation, and the motivations behind those decisions. In a scholarly edition of a literary system, the curated text is a dataset carefully gathered and edited by expert hands, with relationships and contextual information about each text preserved. The data is not scraped by a computer; it is made and organized by a scholar. The *NRD* is a curated edition of the literary system of book reviewing of English novels from the Romantic period, specifically of those published in the *Monthly* and *Critical* Reviews.

Book reviews—specifically individual reviews from Review periodicals in the eighteenth century—resist our study of them through macro or distant reading because reviews are not a flat or linear text; each article reaches out in a constellation connection to other articles, to the world around them. They require "a framework for modeling" that "can support detailed and nuanced representations of literary systems that explore the existence of literary works in the past and support future investigations of those works and systems" for future study.[41] A scholarly edition of a literary system differentiates from the practice of distant reading. As Bode argues, the former has the capability to "outline the relationships between the historical context explored: the disciplinary infrastructure employed in understanding that context; the decisions and selections implicated in creating and remediating that collection; and the additional transformations wrought by the editor's extraction, construction, and analysis of those data."[42] This intervention in generalized quantitative studies or distant reading in humanities is one of data feminism, which Catherine D'Ignazio and Lauren F. Klein argue is "a way of thinking about data, both their uses and their limits, that is informed by direct experience, by a commitment to action, and by intersectional feminist thought."[43]

A scholarly edition of a literary system takes into account the complexities and context behind data, making room for them in our analysis. This is essential when focusing on women and other marginalized individuals and subjects, because "data feminism can help to remind us that before there are data, there are people—people who offer up their experience to be counted and analyzed. . . . There are also, always, people who go uncounted."[44] Novels and periodicals during this period themselves "direct our attention to the collective rather than the singular."[45] The *NRD*, then, is an essential tool for the feminist work of studying eighteenth-century and Romantic reviews of novels, and my building of it aligns with Ozment's insistence that "a feminist scholar will place significance on variances, oddities, and norms that another scholar might not" and build "tools, resources, and lists [that] might be designed to specifically promote work on women and other figures in minority categories of identity and production."[46]

The Novels Reviewed Database, 1790–1820

The work of bibliography has much to teach scholars about overlooked but foundational elements of literary studies. These elements are not invisible but are often taken for granted by many literary scholars who engage with the texts they study only in the edited and affordable editions by Norton, Oxford, Penguin, or Broadview presses. As is true of most eighteenth-century and Romantic periodicals, to date, there is no complete scholarly edition of the *Monthly* or *Critical Review*. A scholarly edition, as Jerome McGann and Paul Eggert outline, is not a reproduced typeset of one version of a work's appearance in print, mirroring that original in its entirety.[47] Access to periodicals in original copies or via textual database provides no scholarly edition, and any who work with periodical originals regularly run into variants—pages missing, advertisements or inserts rarely extant, entire numbers lost, months skipped by editors, and more.

A scholarly edition, however, is a hybrid of many textual variants scattered across multiple editions of the original text, pieced together as a *new* version that, in its exact form, likely never existed before. It is the critical work of the scholar-editor to make these content choices, all grounded in a larger argument about why *this* version of the text should be read. Building a scholarly edition of the literary system of book reviewing during the period when English women novelists dominated the landscape requires feminist scholarship, both by including context in that tool and by attending to the method of its building with transparency.

The *NRD* is devoted singularly to uncovering the narrative of one genre's review criticism. Using multiple hard copies, microfilm, and several digital surrogates of each issue of the *Monthly* and the *Critical* from January 1790 to December 1820, that period identified as the height of women's dominance of novel publishing, the *NRD* is a curated text of each article's criticism of works that the Reviews identified as novels—that is, reviews under the heading of "Novels" in the Monthly Catalogue, reviews that call a work a novel in the body of the review, or a review of a work whose title identifies itself with the word "novel." The *NRD* includes 1,636 book reviews, tracking bibliographical data on 1,215 novels and their publishers and over 445 identified authors. Each review has been tagged for the novel's authorial gender, title genre markers, page space it occupies in the Review, review contributors, and more. Where the *Romantic Women Writers Reviewed* print series and *Women Writers in Review* database pull together reviews of named major women authors across all genres, the *NRD* focuses on novels themselves and does not exclude little-known voices or anonymous authorship.[48]

The *NRD* provides scholars with a transparently created and collated text of novel reviews as these periodicals presented them to the Romantic reading public. It is accompanied by a procedures guide that outlines decisions I made and reasonings behind them for the *NRD*'s data-compilation process. Though as Batchelor notes, "completeness is always an illusion in periodical studies," I have collated the *NRD* through consultation of multiple copies of each issue to attempt a complete and continuous edition.[49] The *NRD* provides an accessible volume of novel reviews in a Microsoft Excel file that, with the procedures guide, is deposited open-access on *BibSite.org*. It is my hope that this will prevent scholars from needing to reproduce the labor of scanning or manually entering data from bibliographic references, multiplying the opportunity for introducing error into that data. Orr, Gamer, Hudson, and countless others have laboriously recounted, reentered, and retracked data from various print bibliographies simply because an authoritative electronic file is not made freely or publicly available.

The *NRD* bridges the gap between sprawling, organized, well-funded (for labor, web hosting, constant maintenance, etc.) digital references, like the wonderful *British Fiction Database, 1800–1829*, and very useful research and datasets that languish, like Michael Treadwell's invaluable notes and genealogies on British publishers, in desks or on computers.[50] The database format enables a re-creation of some contemporary reading practices, outlined in Chapter 1, to aid scholars in contextualizing reviews and Review practices in relation to Romantic era issues of authorial gender, genre, and the literary marketplace. This monograph serves as what usually constitutes the introduction and critical arguments *around* a scholarly edition, grounding the text itself in historical and methodological context. With the availability of the *NRD* as an Excel file alongside this book, scholars, especially those without advanced coding skills to extract data from various digital resources, are provided with the edited text of the reviews *and* an accessible tool for reading and using that data.

Though due to time and labor constraints, the scope of this work only considers the *Critical* and the *Monthly*, readers can and should think about how these data, and the context and conclusions surrounding them, can helpfully bridge to other periodicals. Indeed, it is my hope that future scholars will expand the *NRD* to include other periodicals and perhaps other genres under review. Ina Ferris works through the arguments I make here about the gendered nature of reviewing practices toward novels in particular into the Romantic period, specifically focusing on these elements in the *Edinburgh Review (1802–1929)*, *Quarterly Review (1809–1967)*, *British Critic (1793–1843)*, and other periodicals that printed (or reprinted) book reviews between their pages.[51] These later Reviews, however, take up an op-ed essayistic style of reviewing similar to the modern practices as opposed to the report-and-assessment style of the earlier *Monthly* and *Critical* and therefore cannot be considered equal base units in the *NRD*'s literary system. They do, however, continue the spirit of these practices and perpetuate the gendered rhetoric well into the twentieth century, further spreading the many-pronged and long-reaching effects of the Reviews on literary history.

The *NRD* helps us get at questions that previous bibliographies could not. This is because the Reviews are not just a list of works published; they instead offer us the opportunity to view literary history through the circulation of ideas *about* that literature. Each novel was read by a multitude of English readers, as were the Reviews. Those works of fiction and the literary criticism about their dominantly feminine authorship circulated through the system of book reviewing in England and went on to influence canon formation and gendered scholarship about these women writers for centuries. Above all, this book and the *NRD* are seated in questions of gender: What was the contemporary critical conversation about the novel by women? How did women novelists participate in this conversation? How were their works influenced by book reviews? Which authors were affected? How does evidence of this influence show up in our modern literary canon? To what degree did Review criticism make assumptions about authors' and readers' gender? Were they accurate? What were the implications of these assumptions? Did criticism of novels recognize female and male authors equally? How was authorial gender represented to novel-reading audiences? How did history receive these novels and authors? Were they remembered or forgotten? How was their gender a driving factor in the ways they were read, remembered, or forgotten? How does gender influence the ways modern scholarship tries to study writers of the past and a genre defined by women? How does gender influence research studies of those subjects today? Without an appropriate tool, it has been impossible to answer most of these queries.

Simon Eliot and Stephanie Eckroth argue that we need "both broad studies . . . and case studies" to make clear to us the publishing context of the late eighteenth and early nineteenth centuries.[52] And Kate Harrington notes of gender in data analysis that most women resemble most men, and so "the oft cited difference [is] depended on the few and not representative of the many."[53] What follows in this book is a study of each, the many and the few, chapters on methodology and of case studies, which together argue what we stand to gain from using a curated edition of novel reviews to uncover how Romantic women novelists were participating in and critiqued by England's book-reviewing system.

Chapter 1 is a methodological chapter, "Reading the Review Periodical in Eighteenth-Century England," which tackles the questions of what we lose when we cite book reviews via methods that divorce them from their historical context. Specifically, this chapter asks how contemporary readers read and used Reviews. While studies of eighteenth-century and Romantic literature often use review articles to note contemporary reception, Review criticism is not feedback by wider readers. Rather, it is an assessment by one literary critic—or seemingly a group of literary critics—attempting to ground the novel under review in a larger genre genealogy and narrative arc in Britain's literary production. Reviews not only circulated a professional critic's assessment of that text, they also instructed the reading nation on how to interpret and evaluate literature, thus serving as a pedagogical tool. Understanding the context of these periodicals as a whole, then, recasts the tone, rhetoric, and message of each individual review article when read *in* the periodical rather than extracted *from* it. Using extensive material evidence from hard copies of the Reviews, marginalia in novels, and traces left by readers in journals, letters, and pamphlets, I outline two central modes by which eighteenth-century readers encountered Reviews and how the Reviews carefully constructed and managed readerly consumption of their pages. Unfortunately, the digital archiving of these periodicals, which *should* make them more available to scholars, often perpetuates a disassociated reading of their combined pages. By clarifying the context for reading eighteenth-century Reviews through these methods, Chapter 1 calls for a tool to help scholars do such reading ourselves. The *NRD therefore* facilitates a return to contemporary methods of reading.

Chapter 2, "A Dialogue in Print: Reviews and Novel Prefaces," turns to the content of review articles, and returns agency and voice to the women novelists who are the subject of this book. While a mapping of the influence of Review periodicals may seem to situate these women as just that—*subjects* of criticism—they in fact lent their voices to a public-facing print dialogue concerning the formation of the novel and its feminine authorship. The messages in these women's prefaces, introductions, advertisements, and other paratext are often the only extant trace of their voices or authorial experiences left to the historical record. The *NRD* shows that the Reviews not only print their responses to these prefatory declarations, they also reprint excerpts of these prefaces rather than passages from the novels under scrutiny, as was their usual tradition. By doing so, the Reviews expose a dialogue between themselves and novelists, making their conversation accessible even to those contemporary periodical readers who do not procure or peruse the novels themselves. Bringing together for the first time these two genres—prefaces and reviews—this chapter follows the preface–Review dialogue as an ongoing and well-known practice during this period. Identifying eight preface conventions and their relationship to this dialogue, I trace their use through the paratexts of canonical writers like Frances Burney and Charlotte Smith and lesser-known authors such as Anna Maria Porter and Regina Maria Roche, across over 350 prefaces that engaged the Reviews. Unearthing women novelists' participation in this dialogue recasts them as savvy marketers of their own work; they considered themselves professional contributors to the novel's growing legitimacy. Further, this exchange across textual boundaries highlights how the genres were in constant concert with one another; scholarship on the novel and the book market must account for this dialogue in order to understand writing, publishing, reading, and criticism as tandem structures. This chapter enriches our conception of women novelists from this period as spirited authors of their own prosperity, cheekily navigating the Reviews' attempts to cast them as simpering happenstance authors.

Chapter 3, "The Rise and Fall of Charlotte Smith, Novelist," shows the long-lasting influence the Reviews have on our modern literary canon using power-house women writers as case studies. Smith was recognized by the Reviews as a peer to the celebrated Frances Burney and Ann Radcliffe. Reviews call the three together the "sister queens" of the novel. Tracing Review rhetoric directly from the Romantic era into twentieth-century scholarship, I show the long-lasting influence of the Reviews, using Smith as a stark example. Though her early sentimental novels received extensive praise, in her later fiction, Smith displays her political leanings and experiments with flawed and dynamic characters—a generic turn that the Reviews would not, or could not, condone. I use the *NRD* to track the changing attention the Reviews paid Smith's novels across the 1790s: the fluctuating number of pages, the varying location of reviews, the quality of their evaluation, and their interaction with Smith's prefaces. These changes in Review attention and interaction over the course of a decade effectively removed Smith from the eighteenth-century novel's canon. Even feminist recovery work long perpetuated the Reviews' sidelining of Smith as a novelist, primarily cementing her as a poet in modern anthologies. This case study of one famous, popular, and skilled woman novelist across 200 years of criticism highlights how scholarship today is deeply influenced by the eighteenth-century Reviewing system. Without the *NRD*, such catalysts for Siskin's "Great Forgetting" of women's literary dominance are, like these feminine writers, all but obscured.

It is, of course, important to note that no methodological structure or scholarly research process is without flaws; our resources are filled with human error and biases. Transparency in methodology alone can prevent our reproducing errors of past scholarship. Rather than sweep these blemishes under the rug, my last chapter, "A Study in 55 Novels: Data Trouble and Resistant Narratives in the Novel's History," closely examines those novels that resist the outlined scope, plans, and methodology I used to create the *NRD*. Herein I investigate what these "flaws" tell us about modern scholars' assumptions *about*, or the narratives we force *onto*, literary history, even and perhaps most of all in places where authors or works do not fold neatly into our curated concept of the past. Taking up the 55 novels recorded in the *NRD* that are not catalogued in earlier surveys of the genre, I investigate each work to carve out a series of subgenres and authorships that modern scholars have distinctly pushed outside our fabricated boundaries of the eighteenth-century and Romantic novel. All are dominantly authored by women: juvenile novels, translations, memoirs turned fiction, and more. While quantitative study can highlight large patterns and refocus our attention, it also obscures the smaller populations, perpetuating a mainstream narrative rather than challenging it. The *NRD* enables us to work *through* data trouble, not around it. In this chapter, I trace the stories of two women otherwise obscured by the very data-driven studies that make them visible. These writers are essential voices in the history of the English novel— voices that deeply complicate and diversify how we understand feminine authorship in the Romantic era. These casualties of our biased research methods include a queer author attempting to escape heteronormativity while holding onto motherhood and a disabled woman whose writing leads us to question how our genre expectations for the English novel uphold ableism in genre definitions and modern scholarship.

The following chapters navigate the literary system of book reviewing for the first time in our scholarship on women's novels in the Romantic period. They also expose how our previous understandings of these women's writing, lives, and experiences might be more richly understood during this particularly charged 30 years, the Minerva Press Era, when their literary affluence crested despite the many social constraints that pressed upon women at the time. This combination of methodological starting points and applicable case studies for examining the influence of the book reviewing system on the height of women's novel writing in England is an avenue for reorienting women writers and periodical studies in literary history. The complexity of the careers of little-known and canonical women novelists is brough into focus when we consider this vast system they not only knew about but kept the pulse of, wrote into, manipulated, and, at times, were dragged down by.

CHAPTER ONE

Reading the Review Periodical in Eighteenth-Century England

How did eighteenth-century readers read the Review periodical?[1] Despite their long run across the eighteenth and nineteenth centuries, influence on book production and reception, and impact on reading practices, no work has yet set out to uncover how Review periodicals themselves were consumed. Asking how periodicals were read is a complex question; the answer is both obvious and difficult to ascertain. Because periodicals—and, more specifically, Review periodicals—are still read today, it is easy to assume that our current approach to reading such texts is inherited from past readers. This is likely why little work has been done to expose historical periodical reading customs. And yet it is not because contemporaries read these texts differently than modern consumers that scholars should turn their attention to those practices. Rather, it is important to understand historical reading practices so that scholars are mindful of the way we use Reviews and the reviews in them to make other arguments.

Tracking reading practices is notoriously difficult, and methods for going about such challenging research are varied. For example, William St. Clair relies heavily on publishing records.[2] His readers are those who had access to books, and the crux of his argument depends on changing copyright legislation after the 1774 *Donaldson v. Becket* ruling that loosened the power publishers had to tightly control printing and therefore the availability of texts. St. Clair meticulously counts the number of copies printed, and his research is incredibly valuable, if problematic. Jan Fergus also tackles the question of readers and reading practices with quantitative studies from booksellers' records. She notes who bought or borrowed which books and recognizes problems in such records, especially where women readers are concerned.[3] In this chapter, I examine a full run of both the *Monthly Review* (1749–1845) and the *Critical Review* (1756–1817) in terms of format and structure and turn to firsthand accounts of reading Reviews along with eighteenth-century marginalia to identify the methods contemporary readers used to peruse Review periodicals. These varied pieces of evidence together reveal two types of Review-reading practices that I define and outline: chronicle-style reading and catalogue-style reading.

This is not to say that the following is the only way that readers consumed review articles. Certainly, individual articles were cut out and read separately. It is of this practice that William Cowper wrote to a friend, "I am bound to thank you for preventing Johnson from sending me that bundle of Criticisms," suggesting that having a London contact collect review articles from a variety of journals was commonplace.[4] Readers also likely collected and read review articles from books or scrapbooks. Additionally, reviews were consumed in an extracted form well known to modern readers—reproductions by booksellers on book jackets or advertisements. Articles from the *Monthly* or the *Critical* were regularly reprinted in other periodicals, like the *Literary Intelligencer*, enabling them to reach a wider reading audience. *The Lady's Magazine* was known to reprint excerpts from the Reviews to fill the space in that magazine.[5] But those who read the Review periodical itself, evidence shows, often practiced chronicle- or catalogue-style reading.

The extended titles of the Reviews present an argument for two major ways that they were read by contemporaries, one of which was chronicle-style reading. The *Critical*'s full title situates itself in the mid-eighteenth-century book market, one that already had the *Monthly*. The *Critical Review: or, Annals of Literature. By a Society of Gentlemen* suggests, by taking up the name *Critical Review*, that it is more heavily focused on close evaluation than the *Monthly*. But the subtitle, *Annals of Literature*, points to how the *Critical* was intended to be read.[6] Reviews' monthly installments are part of their annual report on that year's literary production. These monthly issues are, at their core, a collection of publications that are separate but gathered by the Reviews to create a picture or account of literature for that month. The *Critical*'s subtitle, *Annals of Literature*, refers to recorded events in sequence, or a narrative.[7] Like a historian linking otherwise unconnected events to create a chronology, the Reviews link the otherwise independent books published or made popular in a single year by reviewing them—grouping them together to represent a story, or chronicle, of that year's publications.

Reading through a monthly number in a manner similar to reading a traditional book—front to back—is what I term "chronicle-style reading." Starting with the front articles and reading each article in turn, the chronicle-style reader continues through the reviews of books that are otherwise seemingly unconnected or unrelated, until they have read most, or all, of the review articles in the order that they are printed. Chronicle-style reading immerses the reader in the Review's writing style. It makes each issue an individual short narrative while also calling back to earlier issues and connecting consecutive reviews together. This connection, that each review article is part of the story of each issue and each issue a part of the larger narrative of that year's report on new books, is the Reviews' chronicle of books printed in Britain—the "Annals of Literature." Jennie Batchelor argues that magazine and periodical "contents need to be read both synchronically—as items in explicit or implicit conversation with others in the same issue—and diachronically—as items in dialogue with other pieces of content published in multiple issues over time."[8] Often, methods for digitizing periodicals overlook scholars' need to recreate this practice; ProQuest's *British Periodicals Database* catalogues their periodicals by article, sometimes by title, sometimes by an Optical Character Recognition (OCR)–identified page number, meaning OCR software identifies the string of characters representing pagination (often incorrectly). This renders the practice of flipping article by article or page by page accurately almost impossible. In this way, our reliance on digital surrogates for accessing many rare historical periodicals is wholly incompatible with recreating historical reading practices.[9]

The *Monthly*'s extended title also indicates chronicle-style reading: *The Monthly Review. A Periodical Work. Giving An Account, with proper Abstracts of, and Extracts from, the New BOOKS, PAMPHLETS, &c. as they come out.* An "account" can also be a story or statement of events in addition to its more utilitarian meaning as a counting, recording, list, or reckoning.[10] The *Monthly*, as the first Review periodical in England, defines its genre as one that pulls together abstracts of such diverse literatures as "books, pamphlets, &c." to create a narrative of the literature available to British readers right now. The immediacy of these Reviews also speaks to their chronicle-style reading: They are not reviewing older texts, attempting to construct a genealogy of literature, but rather offering a sequence of publications "as they come out." The Review offered itself up as middleman, the historian or reporter who gathered information and wrote out an interpretation for the reading public.

Both of these terms, "annals" and "account," however, also denote counting or lists. An "annal" can be "the record or entry of a single year"; an account can be "counting, reckoning, enumeration."[11] In addition to functioning as chronicles of England's literary world, the Reviews were a compendium of books published and indexed for later use as references. These nuanced titles illustrate two lives of the Review periodical—its immediate life, read moments after it is received or purchased, and its long-term life, bound, saved, and referred to by readers for years to come. This second part of the Review's life initiates a use of the periodical as a database, a catalogue-style reading.

Catalogue-style reading differs from chronicle reading in several ways but might appear the most closely related to the selective way scholars commonly use eighteenth-century Reviews now. Catalogue-style reading is when a reader seeks out a particular review article and reads only that review or a small selection of reviews without perusing the entirety of the issue within which it appears. This practice also suggests some distance of time from when the Review issue was first published, whereas chronicle-style reading suggests a more immediate interaction with the Review, when a reader first came into contact with the publication. Catalogue-style reading enhances the longevity of the Reviews' material lives. While it is tempting to categorize the Reviews as ephemeral because they are periodicals, the inclusion of tables of contents, indices to volumes, and footnotes referring readers to other reviews/issues serves to instruct consumers in using the Review for extended periods of time. This assumes that readers are preserving the Reviews. Indeed, circulating libraries boast long runs of the Reviews in their advertised collections. For example, when the Bristol Library Society published a catalogue advertising books available to subscribers, it included the *Critical Review* from July 1773 to August 1797, with the first and second series separately listed.[12] Personal libraries also included copies of the Reviews, as demonstrated by the sale catalogue for the library of politician and businessman George Galwey Mills, which lists "The Critical Review, from the Beginning in 1756 to 1793, inclusive, 79 vol. bound," among its volumes.[13] These holdings indicate readers preserving the Reviews, illustrating the Reviews' accessibility for catalogue-style reference far after their original publication. And while their existence alone in these public and private library collections attests to the extended lives of the Reviews as reading material long past their printing, it is the combination of the Reviews' textual format with rare personal records of reading habits that verifies the contemporary use of these two reading styles.

Chronicle-Style Reading

The consistency of the Reviews' format over their entire publication periods serves as an indicator that they intended or expected chronicle-style reading. "Periodicals (like dramas) are particularly aware of and dependent upon intercourse with their audience in order to justify continued existence," Manushag Powell reminds us; "why else their careful adherence to particular patterns in their first numbers?"[14] And the *Monthly* and the *Critical* do strictly adhere to their reviewing and layout patterns for almost 100 years. Each issue's front 40 to 60 pages reliably feature longer essay-style reviews that include excerpts from the scrutinized text, which are then followed by a Monthly Catalogue where shorter reviews are divided by genre. This consistency illustrates an unwillingness on the part of the Reviews to disrupt the consumer's reading practices.

Placing the most important review as the first article of the issue indicates an expectation of chronicle-style reading on the part of the Reviews' consumers. The relative location of a review within individual issues, then, signaled that work's importance in the hierarchy of published literature. The Review places the article about the most valued or important work first so that their chronicle-style reader will have immediate access to it. These first reviews are of new editions of works by established or canonical authors, such as *Miscellaneous Pieces, in Prose and Verse* by Jonathan Swift (*Monthly* Jan 1790) or *The Works of Alexander Pope, Esq.* (*Monthly* Aug 1797), review articles that stretch across multiple issues like *Dr. Burney's General History of Music* (*Monthly* Dec 1789 continued to Jan and Feb 1790) or Sir Walter Scott's *Rokeby: a Poem* (*Monthly* Feb 1813 continued to Mar 1813), historical works like the expensive quarto edition of *The History of Great Britain from the Death of Henry VIII to the Accession of James VI of Scotland to the Crown of England* by James Pettit Andrews (*Monthly* Mar 1797), travel narratives like William Wittman's *Travels in Turkey, Asia-Minor, Syria, and across the Desert to Egypt* (*Monthly* Jun 1804), current events like Helen Maria Williams's *Letters containing a Sketch of the Scenes which passed in various Departments in France during the Tyranny of Robespierre* (*Critical* Jan 1796) or *The History of the Rise, Progress, and Accomplishment of the Abolition of the African Slave-Trade by British Parliament* by Thomas Clarkson (*Monthly* Apr 1809), or reports such as the *Philosophical Transactions of the Royal Society of London* (*Critical* Jun 1796). These first articles are often lengthy and demand time and attention from readers. The essay style of these longer reviews was better suited to chronicle-style reading.

Review articles in this front section begin with an introduction, offer summary and criticism, provide excerpts from the work under review, and end with a conclusion either recommending or condemning the work. This essayistic review format promotes and expects a chronicle-style reading practice. Each introduction gives general statements on the author or the work at hand and situates the work in that author's corpus. A review will often remind the reader of the periodical's past criticism and overall evaluation of the author. This style in the introductory paragraph serves to connect an article in one issue to previous issues that feature reviews of the author's work and assume a chronicle-style reading practice on the part of a reader who has perused said earlier issues. The periodical, then, expected both reading styles to be practiced in tandem.

The *Critical's* review of Ann Radcliffe's *The Mysteries of Udolpho* in their August 1794 issue serves as an example of the Review expecting chronicle-style reading (Fig. 1.1). Even 38 years after the *Critical's* debut, the periodical still follows the aforementioned format conducive to chronicle-style reading. However, a regular Review reader would have found it surprising to see a novel in the feature first review location. Across the 30 years that this book considers, from 1790 to 1820, *Udolpho* is the only novel to appear in the feature first-review slot of an issue in either the *Critical* or the *Monthly*, and its critic confronts this turn from convention, explaining the review's location by paralleling Radcliffe to Shakespeare in their opening lines. The review offers an epigraph, from Thomas Gray's ode to Shakespeare in his "Progress of Poesy": "Thine too these golden keys, immortal boy! / This can unlock the gates of joy, / Of horror, that and thrilling fears, / Or ope the sacred source of sympathetic tears."[15]

The epigraph is then explained in the review's opening lines noting that "though perhaps to no other mortal has [the muse] been so lavish of her gifts [as to Shakespeare], the keys referring to the third line Mrs. Radcliffe must be allowed to be completely in possession of." Borrowing Gray's lines, the review declares that the muse has bestowed on this particular novelist the twin literary powers of "horror" and "thrilling fears." With this comparison, the review justifies Radcliffe's placement as the lead review in the issue. Situating Radcliffe in the English literary canon beside Shakespeare, the Review is assuming chronicle-style reading on the part of its audience. The opening lines reassure the reader that Radcliffe deserves the spotlight review location, and then goes on in its introduction to connect the novel to its author's corpus. "All those who have

The Mysteries of Udolpho, a Romance; interspersed with some Pieces of Poetry. By Ann Radcliffe, Author of the Romance of the Forest, &c. 4 Vols. 12mo. 1l. Boards. Robinsons. 1794.

'THINE too these golden keys, immortal boy!
    This can unlock the gates of joy,
Of horror, that and thrilling fears,
Or ope the sacred source of sympathetic tears.'

Such were the presents of the Muse to the infant Shakspeare, and though perhaps to no other mortal has she been so lavish of her gifts, the keys referring to the third line Mrs. Radcliffe must be allowed to be completely in possession of. This, all who have read the Romance of the Forest will willingly bear witness to. Nor does the present production require the name of its author to ascertain that it comes from the same hand. The same powers of description are displayed, the same predilection is discovered for the wonderful and the gloomy—the same mysterious terrors are continually exciting in the mind the idea of a supernatural appearance, keeping us, as it were, upon the very edge and confines of the world of spirits, and yet are ingeniously explained by familiar causes; curiosity is kept upon the stretch from page to page, and from volume to volume, and the secret, which the reader thinks himself every instant on the point of penetrating, flies like a phantom before him, and eludes his eagerness till the very last moment of protracted expectation. This art of escaping the guesses of the reader has been improved and brought to perfection along with the reader's sagacity; just as the various inventions of locks, bolts, and private drawers, in order to secure, fasten, and hide, have always kept pace with the ingenuity of the pickpocket and housebreaker, whose profession it is to unlock, unfasten, and lay open what you have taken so much pains to conceal. In this contest of curiosity on one side, and invention on the other, Mrs. Radcliffe has certainly the advantage. She delights in concealing her plan with the

Figure 1.1. The Critical Review 2nd ser., 11.

read the Romance of the Forest will willingly bear witness to" Radcliffe's prowess where horror is concerned. Here the Review (or the authors of the review articles) declares itself to be among "those who have read" Radcliffe's last novel, and indeed they were. *The Romance of the Forest* received a favorable review in the *Critical*'s April 1792 issue (also in the front section, though it was the fourteenth instead of the first article).

Following the introduction that situates Radcliffe's novel, the review moves on to evaluating the work at hand. It compliments Radcliffe's skill at writing about mysteries and imagines Radcliffe as a writer: "[The author] seems to amuse herself with saying, 'Now you think you have me, but I shall take care to disappoint you.'"[16] This intimacy with Radcliffe that the Review assumes by putting haughty words in her mouth comes from its familiarity with her past works and appreciation of the present one. It praises her landscape description and characters and makes only small notice of "little defects, which impartiality obliges us to notice." The review does not attempt to describe the story, as that would "[destroy] the pleasure of the reader," though an extensive excerpt is included.[17] This conversational care of the reader's pleasures hints at a relationship the periodical has nurtured with its audience across a chronicle-style reading of many articles, particularly those reviewing the works of this author.

The review ends with a conclusion. This outline—an introduction, a criticism, an excerpt, and a conclusion—encourages readers to peruse the article rather than to skip to the excerpt or read only the conclusion. The review's assumption that its reader has read the article in order is evident in the conclusion, which further imagines dialogue between Radcliffe and themselves: "If, in consequence of the criticisms impartiality has obliged us to make upon this novel, the author should feel disposed to ask us, Who will write a better?" After speaking for Radcliffe, the Review answers for its chronicle-style readers, who have become the voyeurs to the Review's imagined relationship with that author: "We boldly answer her, *Yourself*."[18] This conclusion not only invites Radcliffe to write more novels with the promise of better reviews, it also invites Review readers to stay tuned for future glimpses of Radcliffe's work. This conclusion also recommends *The Mysteries of Udolpho* to the *Critical*'s readers in an almost sensual manner. The italics of *"Yourself"* insinuate a bold whisper against the ear of the author (and, by proxy, the reader). The review's reflective style, imagined dialogues, and paralleling of the reviewers themselves with the readers reflect the assumption that those readers have read the entirety of the article in chronicle-style practice.

Chronicle-style reading also connects articles across multiple issues of the Reviews through correspondence sections. While periodicals commonly include a short question or two in this section, in a Review, this extended discussion calls back to the review article itself, illustrating a chronicle-style reading that connects one issue to another. The *Critical* demonstrates its expectation that readers are practicing chronicle-style reading when they offer an extensive correspondence response at the end of the Monthly Catalogue three months after publishing their review of *The Mysteries of Udolpho*.[19] The correspondent seems to have believed the review contained too much criticism of Radcliffe's novel, so the *Critical* reassures them that they "have no hesitation in pronouncing it 'The most interesting novel in the English language.'" Throughout their response, the Review refers to its previous review article. This correspondence response is one and a half pages long—too significant of a space in the periodical for the Review to have published it expecting it to speak to only one reader. The lengthy response, then, invites the chronicle-style reader into an extended discussion on Radcliffe's novel, assuming all the while the reader is familiar with the original review.

Further evidence that the Reviews expected chronicle-style reading practices is indicated in review articles within the same issue that are dependent on one another for clarity. In the January 1809 Monthly Catalogue of the *Monthly Review*, the ability to understand the review of Agnes Musgrave's *William de Montfort; or the Sicilian Heiress* is dependent on the reader having read the review printed above it, that of Mary Pickar's *The Castle of Roviego* (Fig. 1.2). The reviewer, whom Benjamin Christie Nangle has identified as Thomas Ogle, argues that Pickar's setting in a rambling castle would be better understood if the author had provided her readers with an "architectural plan."[20] The next review printed directly below that of *The Castle of Roviego* gives no plot summary or evaluation of the work as a whole. Instead, Ogle's review refers directly to the previous article, stating: "If a ground-plan was necessary to the preceding work, the present stands as much in need of a genealogical table."[21] The construction of these reviews as interdependent necessitated their being printed consecutively. An equally short review could have been crafted to cite the need of a genealogical chart for *William de Montfort* without referring to the previous review, but it was not.

Other modes of referring back to previous reviews are more subtle, such as the review of *Durval and Adelaide*, which notes that the novel, "like the former, is translated from the French," referring to the review of *Louis de Boncaeur* printed on the preceding page.[22] These reviews were also both written by one person, Arthur Aikin. Such a willingness to write a review dependent on the

MONTHLY CATALOGUE, *Poetry*.   101

NOVELS.

Art. 24. *The Castle of Roviego;* or Retribution. A Romance.
By Mary Pickar. 12mo. 4 Vols. Booth.

On endeavouring to retrace the impressions made on us by the perusal of these volumes, nothing seems to strike us more forcibly than the confusion which we experienced from the intricacies in the building of this old Castle. We are therefore led to suggest that, in cases like the present, it might perhaps add to the interest or at least facilitate the comprehension of the story, if the writer would subjoin an architectural plan.

Art. 25. *William De Monfort;* or the Sicilian Heiresses. By
Agnes Musgrave. 12mo. 3 Vols. Richards.

If a ground-plan was necessary to the preceding work, the present stands as much in need of a genealogical table.

Figure 1.2. The Monthly Review 2nd ser., 58 (January 1809): 101. Copy held by University of Minnesota.

previous article having been read shows a clear expectation that the reader will proceed through the issue using chronicle-style reading. In addition to structural evidence within the Reviews illustrating that they anticipated chronicle-style reading, individual reflections on the Reviews from letters, journals, and print pamphlets confirm these expectations. These brief comments about the Reviews reveal the reading practices that led to such conclusions or beliefs on the part of their authors.

Habitual reading of the Reviews is an indicator of chronicle-style reading. A regular chronicle-style reading of Review issues made a reader aware of the Review's structure and of its recurring types of criticism. Pamphlets such as *An appendix to the occasional critic, in which the remarks on that performance in the critical and monthly reviews are examined* (1757) and *The Battle of the Reviews* (1760), which records a war between the *Critical* and the *Monthly* in the manner of Swift's *The Battle of the Books*, are evidence of a reading public familiar enough with the Reviews to understand their criticism and to parody their identities for a mock war. Unfortunately named pamphlet author Joseph Wimpey reveals his reading practices in *A Letter to the Authors of the Monthly Review Occasioned by their Remarks on Two Pamphlets lately published* (1771). Before launching into his criticism of how the *Monthly* treated his works, Wimpey states: "Soon after your REVIEW for the monthly of August was published, I was asked if I had read your last REVIEW; I answered yes, and that I commonly allowed myself that pleasure." Confirming that he specifically consumed the reviews of his own works, Wimpey also herein discloses that he was a regular, or "common" consumer of the Reviews. Wimpey's pamphlet, which responds line by line to the review of his earlier pamphlets on the price of corn, certainly shows his familiarity with the reviews of his publications. Though it is possibly false flattery, this admission of regular Review reading and that he was aware of the Reviews' tendency to "correct any mistakes" of a work under scrutiny points to Wimpey practicing chronicle-style reading and is a rare instance of published review-reading practice.[23]

This is not to say that in chronicle-style reading, every review in every issue is read. Rather, chronicle-style reading evidence tells us that the Reviews at least expected some kind of continuity in their consumers' reading practices. And this expectation implies that people were reading the Review periodical itself to consume the reviews. Cowper complains that even tradespeople are such regular readers of the *Monthly Review* that they could encounter a poor review of his *Poems by William Cowper* (1782) and be influenced to dislike it: "Here are Watchmakers, who themselves are Wits, and who, at present, perhaps think me one. Here is a carpenter and a baker, and not to mention others, here is your Idol Mr. Teedon, whose smile is fame. All these read the *Monthly Review*, and all these will set me down for a dunce if those Terrible Critics show them the example."[24] Cowper's statement that watchmakers, carpenters, and bakers all "read the *Monthly Review*" does not refer to select or occasional reading of Reviews. The blanket statement that they "*read* the *Monthly Review*" [emphasis mine] implies regularity or habit, and an expectation that they will encounter the review of his *Poems*, the fifth article in the *Monthly*'s October 1782 issue.[25] These habitual reading practices, which the Reviews depended on and expected, influenced the aforementioned setup of each review article and of the hierarchy of articles within each issue.

Chronicle-style reading also familiarized readers with the rhetoric and criticisms of the Reviews. The Reviews' constant harping on the grammar and style of an author's writing was well known. This tendency led Carol Percy to dub the Reviews "language guardians," and a chronicle-style reading practice exposed this repeated criticism to Review readers.[26] When lawyer George Wilson writes to Jeremy Bentham on June 5, 1788, "enclos[ing] part of the Monthly Review which will probably give you some pleasure," he includes the caveat "notwithstanding the impertinent remarks on the Style at the end."[27] Wilson knows that comments on grammar were common in the *Monthly* and to be made little of. He even notes the location of these types of criticisms—"at the end" of the review article. This note to their location indicates Wilson's having read review articles through to the end in chronicle-style reading practice.

Hester [Thrale] Piozzi would later complain of the exhaustive catalogue the *Critical Review* made of factual, printing, and grammatical errors in her world history, *Retrospection* (1801).[28] Their entire review of her work is a complaint of errors, but their comment on language is near the end. Considering that economy of page space in the Reviews induced reviewers to be concise in their criticisms and rely on excerpts as examples of positive or negative critiques rather than exhaustively laying them out for readers, their excessive use of space for grammatical and language corrections is significant. The *Critical* devotes an entire page to recording errors in Piozzi's work, including four lines on one error. The review exclaims: "As Mrs. Piozzi has written on English synonyms, we are surprised to see the word *disannul*, p. 485." Here they cite the page number, presumably so that Piozzi can make corrections, which they give to her: "As to annul is to extinguish, to disannul must signify to replace, or just the reverse of the sense in which Mrs. Piozzi uses it."[29] Piozzi takes to the press to give the *Critical* a taste of their own medicine, crafting an inventory of the errors in their review in her letter published in *The Gentleman's Magazine* a few months later.[30] Both Wilson's and Piozzi's familiarity with the Review's trend in cataloguing errors in language, and where they are located in review articles is indicative of a widespread use of chronicle-style reading. It is clear then that regular or habitual reading of the Reviews made their pet peeve of grammatical errors common knowledge to contemporary readers and writers alike.

Literary scholars and book historians today seldom take up reading the Reviews in a chronicle-style manner. This is the result of two problems: The first involves our classing the Review periodical as a secondary genre operating on the periphery of literary culture and, because it is dependent on the publication of *other* texts, seeing it only as a supplement to the works it reviews rather than as a text and genre worthy in its own right of our attended study. The second is the relative inaccessibility of historical periodicals to researchers today. This book and the *Novels Reviewed Database (NRD)* take steps to rectify both of these obstacles. As chronicle-style reading shows us, a contemporary novel-reader holding their issue of a Review periodical over their breakfast table could navigate through the physical space of the feature articles, perhaps stopping to enjoy a long review of Frances Burney's work and eventually skimming over the genre headers in the Monthly Catalogue until their eyes rested on the short notices of prose fiction. The tangible navigation of the periodical—the turning of leaves and the wandering of eyes over pages—consistently reinforces the position of the novel in the wider and hierarchical genre network of the period. And while the *NRD* is a curated dataset of the reviews of novels, and only of their criticism,[31] it offers bibliographical details in each entry that enable a user to triangulate material elements of the review's position in a monthly issue, its relationship to other articles, and its visual makeup on the page. These features of the *NRD* work to ensure that central material and cultural elements that weigh on the individual articles do not disappear into the larger dataset, thereby making invisible their influence or producing false correlations by obscuring their relevance. But after an initial chronicle-style reading of an issue had concluded and the number was placed on a shelf or bound up with other issues into a fine volume, how did eighteenth-century readers continue to consume the Review periodical?

Catalogue-Style Reading

We struggle to fit periodicals into generic categories of literature because they hold so many of them simultaneously—poetry, essays, news, engravings, eulogies. Reviews are no different, and indeed while featuring a multitude of authors who wrote the original texts reviewed and excerpted, Reviews also include the invisible and anonymous writing of multiple critics' hands.[32] A single review article may feature a work's author (in excerpts from the original text), multiple reviewers, corrections by the periodical's editor, a work's extended titles, and comments from the publisher or bookseller. And while the Reviews have a printed list order, a linear progression from the first article in the first issue, reaching across subsequent monthlies, they also provide a form for each item under review as a means of data collection—a catalogue.

One might ask why I do not explore the Reviews as an archive. This is because the Reviews are not archives; they are not interested in storing, preserving, or representing originals—that is, the original work under review. Further, they have no *archivist*—nobody is organizing and shepherding the articles and their Review containers through collection, preservation, and use—and while it may seem that the Reviews are doing that labor themselves, it is the human element of an archivist that actually defines an archive. Any metaphorical use of the concept discounts and strips acknowledgment of the years (centuries) of labor that curators of those collections perform. Rather, the Reviews outline a series of data points for each work, recording them faithfully in a form/format and then, like all databases or catalogues, turning to interpretation. Therefore, as Kenneth M. Price reminds us, "a database is not an undifferentiated sea of information out of which structure emerges. Argument is always there from the beginning in how those constructing a database choose to categorize information."[33] Reviews are not blind and indiscriminate collections of texts published in England. All works published are not represented. Rather, the Reviews make an argument about quality, importance, contribution, and canon with each work they recognize. When the *Critical* publishes its review of Radcliffe's *The Mysteries of Udolpho* as its lead article in the August 1794 issue, it legitimizes the genre as moving from base literature to noteworthy and recognizes Radcliffe's work as an example of what a "high" novel should be. The Reviews create through their articles their own dataset, which I curate in the *NRD*. Such a database allows me to curate a scholarly text of the reviewing system that enables modern chronicle- and catalogue-style reading.

The data-entry form for each record in the Reviews database is easy to identify—and in this way, they do differ from other types of periodicals, like the essay format of *The Spectator* or compilation journals like the *Gentleman's Magazine*. Each "record" or review article includes the following fields: title, author, number of volumes, publisher, size, price, binding, year of publication, criticism, and excerpt (Figs. 1.1 and 1.2). The Reviews faithfully enter these data points for every record in their system. The ordering of reviews from most to least important in each issue and presentation of feature articles with essay-style formats that included introductions, progressive commentary, and conclusions point to the Reviews' expectation of chronicle-style reading, which trained readers in their database hierarchy cataloguing system. This also therefore prepared readers for catalogue-style reading. But a database is also a dismantling of structure—of chronology, of categories. Bi- and later triannually, the Reviews published indices to their volumes for consumers to bind with their issues. The indices offer various ways to categorize reviews (records) other than by the value hierarchy suggested in their linear placement within each issue or the genre categories that confine them in the Monthly Catalogue. The indices offer a multiplicity of axes through which readers can access or search a review and/or a work under review.[34]

Both the *Monthly Review* and the *Critical Review* include a table of contents for each issue, a cataloguing progression that suggests that each volume index is an aggregation of the entries from each issue's table of contents. The Reviews were not merely cataloguing contents, however; they were making meaning. By building structures like tables of contents, article numbers, and indices into their format, the Reviews were, as James Mussell calls it, "writing the future of their archival afterlives"—that is, they were outlining future reading practices.[35]

And while the Reviews' very recognition of a publication preserved evidence of its existence—now sometimes the only evidence of existence for works where no copies survive—they presented another argument in their indexing. The *Monthly* eventually settled on the section heading "Index to the REMARK-ABLE PASSAGES in this volume." In early issues, however, the claim that the index featured only references to "remarkable passages" is missing. Indeed, early volumes of the *Monthly* title their "INDEX." with a hard stop and on the next line give these directions to their reader: "N.B. To find any particular BOOK, or PAMPHLET, see the TABLE OF CONTENTS, prefixed to the Volume."

This select indexing of "remarkable passages," whether indicated or not, is another organization system, another argument built into the collection of review articles bound together in the Review database. Readers who explored the *Monthly*'s volumes beyond their immediate material lives as separate issues could search for a specific work only if they knew the original month and year during which it was reviewed. Otherwise, they were more likely to find top-tier, "remarkable" works, because the index functioned as a database "browse" feature rather than a comprehensive "search" option. For example, regular readers of the *Monthly* might encounter the review of Thomas Holcroft's translation of Frederic Leopold Count Stolberg's *Travels Through Germany, Switzerland, Italy, and Sicily*, featured in the prestigious front section of the August 1797 issue. They could find it cross-listed in the table of contents under "Stolberg, Travels," or "Holcroft, Translation of Stolberg's Travels," but not under "Travels." But it was not found at all in the index, because while in August the Reviews thought it worthy of a longer review than the Monthly Catalogue could offer, by the end of the year, it was not deemed so great in comparison to the other "remarkable" pieces in that volume.

The *Critical*'s practices initially mirrored those of the *Monthly* but evolved as the Review attempted to be more comprehensive and judicious than its competitor. At its mid-century inception, it included an index that featured authors and subjects but very few titles. Later, the index became more specific. Whereas the *Monthly* evolved to index only "remarkable passages," the *Critical* devoted itself to a fuller scope—an "alphabetical index to the Author's Names and Ti-tles of Books." The table of contents and index for each issue and volume make both Reviews "usable as soon as [they begin] to exist," and the continued use of an outlined format leads readers to "take as a given that the data will con-tinue to proliferate, potentially indefinitely."[36] The searchability of these indi-ces facilitates a catalogue-style reading.

The stylistic format of the Reviews also attests to an expectation of the catalogue style of reading. Each issue serves as a narration that immediately imparts the story of the British book market to the chronicle-style reader. That issue is then deposited with previous issues, and its role moves from being an active voice of the book market to a passive repository of Britain's publication history. St. Clair notes of Reviews that "by dividing their notices of recent books in accordance with the categories used in booksellers' and library catalogues . . . they helped to entrench the ways into which knowledge, as well as texts, was divided and presented."[37] This is highlighted in the Monthly Catalogues, where texts are subdivided by genre.

Evidence of catalogue-style reading by those who returned to the Reviews can be glimpsed in contemporary marginalia in the British Library's copy of Charlotte Smith's *Ethelinde, or the Recluse of the Lake* (1789), written horizontally on the verso of the short title page. Scrawled near the top of the page is a citation for a review of Smith's novel: "See Monthly Review for June 1790, page 161. Enlarged No. 2" (Fig. 1.3). This citation prompts readers of that novel to practice catalogue-style reading by pulling the *Monthly* issue that featured *Ethelinde*'s review and expanding their reading of the novel to include its critical reception. The exactness of this citation—its inclusion of the series ("Enlarged No. 2") and the page number—illustrates an expectation that other readers of this copy of *Ethelinde* will, and should, reference the review as part of their reading experience. Further, it suggests that they had access to the Review in order to reference it, implying that both the novel and a run of the *Monthly Review* (possibly both the old and new series, since that detail is noted) were held in the individual's library.

Written in the same hand below this citation is a quote taken from that review and a seemingly personal assessment of the novel. Including not the first lines but rather an excerpt from the second page of the five-page front-section feature *Ethelinde* received in the *Monthly*, the note reads, "Ethelinde is a very Phœnix—like Richardson's Grandison far too excellent—far above the standard of Nature.—a Woman without a fault, or a single Imperfection, is not to be found in this World, any more than such a Man as Grandison—their Examples are therefore useless."[38] It is not an exact excerpt; the copied passage leaves out a sentence printed in the review. After characterizing Ethelinde as a phoenix, the *Monthly* states, "She appears indeed to be 'all that painting can express, or youthful poets fancy when they love.' Such an object is undoubtedly enchanting." (Box 1.1)[39] The note writer skips over this sentence and records a variation of the review's next sentence, which compares Ethelinde to the main character from Samuel Richardson's *The History of Sir Charles Grandison* (1753).

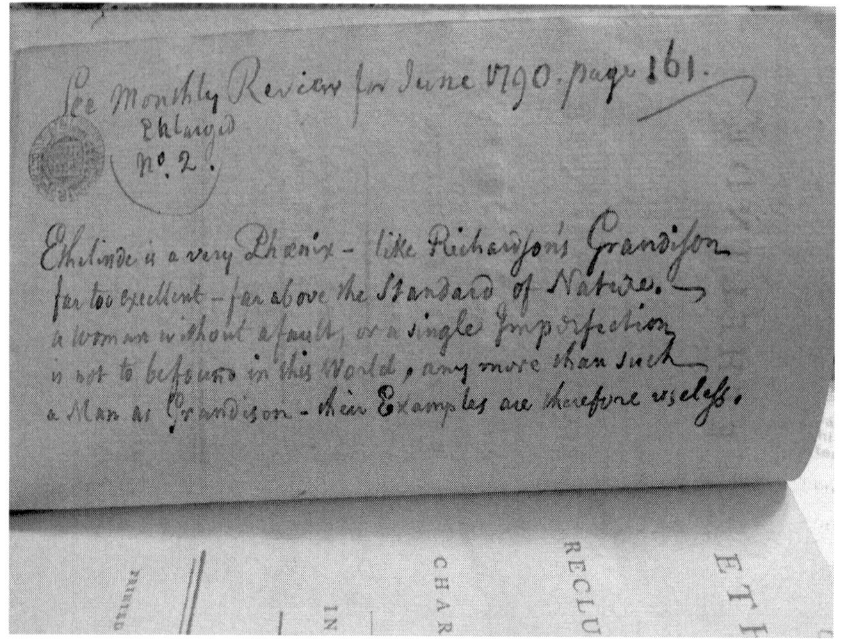

Figure 1.3. Verso of short title of *Ethelinde, or Recluse of the Lake* (1789), vol. 1, from the *British Library.*

BOX I.I

Ethelinde, the lovely, the virtuous Ethelinde, is a very phœnix. She appears indeed to be "all that painting can express, or youthful poets fancy when they love." Such an object is undoubtedly enchanting: but, like Richardson's Grandison, she is far too excellent: far above the standard of nature. A woman, without a fault, without a single imperfection, is no more to be found in this world—whatever *Strephan* may urge to the contrary—than is a man of the same description; and it should be remembered, that, in performances like the present, Nature, dear goddess! is ever to be kept in view.

The Monthly Review 2nd ser., 2 (January 1790) review of Charlotte Smith's Ethelinde, 162. Source text from the University of Missouri Special Collections.

Their choice of this passage to partially reproduce in their copy of *Ethelinde* illustrates the reader had enough access to the Review to cite the exact article down to the issue and page number. The inexact reproduction of the *Monthly*'s review perhaps suggests that the quote was penned from memory, but the exactitude of the citation above it indicates more likely that the writer was copying parts of the review and including a personal assessment of Smith's novel. This particular marginalia demonstrates the material impact of the Review's early mission of giving an account of a work so that readers could make their own conclusion. The *Monthly* gives Smith's *Ethelinde* a positive evaluation, yet the marginalia review in this copy ends with a reflection on *Ethelinde* and *Sir Charles Grandison*'s perfectly formed characters: "Their Examples are therefore useless."

By comparing *Ethelinde* to Richardson's *Grandison*, the Review also evaluates genre across the century. It is perhaps this comparison that specifically draws the note writer to include such a passage in their book. In preparing for and expecting catalogue-style reading, Reviews take on the role of providing readers with an overview of past trends in literature, establishing how recent texts fit into those trends. They do so by referencing already well-established literature, like Richardson's novels, and by identifying literary trends as they emerge. For example, in their 1797 review of *Azemia; A Descriptive and Sentimental Novel*, the *Monthly* states: "The remarks which occurred to us lately in reviewing an ingenious Rhapsodical Romance entitled 'Modern Novel-writing, by the Right Hon. Harriet Marlow,' will apply, with very little variation, to the present production; which seems, in no small degree, an imitation of Lady Harriet's performance.*" The *Monthly* does not need to repeat the points they had "lately" made about Marlow's work. The periodical treats their review of Marlow's novel published a full four years earlier (May 1793) as if it were an earlier chapter in the chronicle of literature in Britain. This practice speaks to their habitual, chronicle-style reading audience. But the Review also provides a footnote to their reference, "*See Review, N.S. vol.xx.p.477"; this data point dispatches people on a catalogue-style reading search of the Review's corpus if they have not seen the review of Marlow or need a refresher.[40] The combination of these two elements in the review of *Azemia* confirms the Reviews' expectation of, and planning for, both chronicle-style and catalogue-style reading practices. It also illustrates the likelihood that both of these reading practices happened in tandem.

In addition to supplementing their articles with previously written articles, as with *Azemia*, the Reviews use these footnote connections across issues and the combined catalogue- and chronicle-style reading practices to add humor to their reviews. For example, in the *Monthly's* 1802 review of Benjamin Frere's *The Man of Fortitude*, the reviewer laments that the author's phantom is nothing but a coach's lamp and so is "sorry to observe that the invention of our writers is nearly exhausted, in their ghostly narrations." The review then offers two suggestions for "Radcliffian" novelists for their fantastic plot devices—the Montgolfier hot air balloon or mermaids. These suggestions are meant to parallel the phantom that turned out to be a coach lamp, but the mermaid suggestion is not immediately clear to a reader consuming only this review article. "Now that we have evidence of the existence of mermaids," the review suggests in a tone seeped with sarcasm, "an ingenious writer might provide himself with a tolerable ghost, to be viewed from the quarter-deck, or cabin-window."[41] This snarky comment on mermaids is footnoted to a review of a medical treatise from the December 1801 issue.

A review of Colin Chisolm's *An Essay on the Malignant Pestilential Fever* is an odd place to find information about mermaids. The reviewer believed so as well, explaining, "This treatise has received so many important additions . . . that we shall deviate from our usual rule of slightly noticing second editions, and bestow on it a rather circumstantial account." We later learn that this introductory explanation for the work's second review is made in jest. After summarizing Chisolm's main argument about the cause of yellow fever, which had not changed since his first edition, the reviewer notes that "he has now added all the information that can be obtained from other publications . . . so that his work really comprises almost every circumstance known respecting the disease." This "added information" is Chisolm's learning of "the famous Mermaid, hitherto considered as a mere creature of the imagination," from the Native peoples of the "West India Islands." Straying from the topic of yellow fever, Chisolm's book provides a lengthy description of the mermaid, given secondhand. The Review excerpts this lengthy description (almost a full page of the review), one it clearly believes has no place in Chisolm's medical text: "We cannot conclude our view of this work without observing, that much of the additional material in the second volume might have been spared."[42] The entire purpose of this review, then, is to excerpt the mermaid portion for the Review readers' entertainment and chastise Chisolm for including it. The repeated references across issues of the Review lay the groundwork for a more robust review of *The Man of Fortitude* in January 1802. This expanded review and the running joke across multiple issues depend both on a reader regularly reading the Review chronicle style and a reader with catalogue-style reading opportunities.

Combined contemporary chronicle- and catalogue-style reading of the Reviews are illustrated in the reading habits of young Joseph Hunter, a sixteen-year-old warehouse apprentice in Sheffield, Yorkshire.[43] He recorded his reading habits in a journal now held at the British Library. Hunter was an avid reader; he regularly took out books from two separate circulating libraries and borrowed reading materials from friends and neighbors. On June 9, 1799, Hunter records in his journal that he "brought . . . from the Chapel Library" the July 1798 issue of *The Analytical Review*. This issue was a year old by the time Hunter borrowed it in order "to read a masterly critique on the 'Castle Spectre,' which I saw performed last winter." He summarizes the article in his journal, noting that the reviewers "allow Mr Lewis no praise at all, indeed plagiarisms (chiefly from Mrs Radcliffe's Publications) are visible on every page."[44] To locate this issue of a Review periodical specifically to read an article on Matthew "Monk" Lewis's gothic drama, Hunter had to do some searching. The *Analytical*, which ran only shortly from 1788 to 1798, adopted the format established by the *Monthly* and the *Critical* of providing indices and tables of contents to help readers return to their saved issues as repositories or databases of British literature using the catalogue-style reading practice. As the issue Hunter checked out was a year old, it is almost certain that he was looking for the review of Lewis's drama specifically, and he would have used the Review's index to find it. The young apprentice, then, is deft in seeking out a review specific to his reading interests.

Conversely, only a few days before this, on June 3, 1799, Hunter "brought the 'Monthly Review' from Miss Haynes." Haynes was a close friend or neighbor to Hunter who regularly lent him periodical reading materials. The *Monthly Review* issue Hunter was reading from was the May 1799 issue. He notes that "this month they review Conder's 'Arrangement of Provincial Coins,' but they do it in a very slight manner." Hunter's calling the May 1799 issue "this month['s]" on June 3 suggests that Haynes had not yet received her June issue of the Review.[45] Hunter here practices catalogue-style reading. The review he notes in his journal, that of James Conder's *An Arrangement of Provincial Coins, Tokens, and Medals*, is featured in the Monthly Catalogue under the "Miscellaneous" genre header. It is likely that Hunter sought out this review specifically, as he recorded reading about Conder's text the previous October in the September 1798 issue of the *Monthly Magazine* in his diary: "The Monthly Magazine contains an account of the publication of that long expected work by Mr Conder of Ipswich, 'an Arrangement of Provincial Coins, Tokens and Medalets Issued in Great Britain, Ireland and the Colonies, Within the Last Twenty Years, from the Farthing to the Penny Size.' Price 7s 6d in Boards. I intend to get this proposed at the Surry Street Library."[46]

Hunter's reading habits show regular contact with periodicals, though he does not always record his process of reading them as clearly as he does other types of books, such as novels. There is no record of his reading practice where the "twelve numbers of the Monthly Magazine that were lent to him by Miss Haynes" are concerned, but such regular borrowing of the same periodical suggests that he did in fact read them.[47] Hunter was reading Review periodicals and the *Monthly Magazine*'s reviews to "decide which texts he wanted to nominate" for his leisure reading time.[48] After reading Isaac Brandon's *Fragments; in the Manner of Sterne* (1797), Hunter "placed it within the critical discourse of the *Monthly Review*," much like the reader of *Ethelinde*, an indicator that he was indeed a regular, chronicle-style reader of that periodical and sought out the review of Lewis's play using a catalogue-style reading practice.[49] Indeed, Stephen Colclough argues that because Hunter regularly recorded what "the *Monthly Review* says" while reading *Fragments*, "he appears to have read the review and text in tandem," like the marginalia in Smith's novel suggests.[50] Hunter's journals offer us the rare opportunity to follow the reading practices of one person. Indeed, we are most indebted to the class position of Hunter that provided him with literacy and just enough leisure time and access to materials to read and consider reading a precious-enough pastime that he deemed it worthy of recording. He is a contemporary reader whose habits modern scholars can now imitate with the use of the *NRD*.

Jerome McGann argues that "We will not design and build effective digital tools . . . unless we work from an adequate understanding of their paper-based inheritance."[51] And indeed, we might better conduct our work if we collapse our understanding of these tools with traditional methods of studying literature and literary criticism and their original material context. Contemporary readers of the Review periodicals had a database at their fingertips—a corpus of valued literature, carefully catalogued and ready for searching. It is perhaps not surprising that the Enlightenment produced a print database considering its widespread interest in quantifying and categorizing information and ideas. It is, however, unreasonable to ask modern scholars to study periodicals, moreover Reviews, using digital tools that cannot be used to reproduce historical reading practices or adapted to expand reliable scholarly resources. Using the *British Periodicals* database, Google Books, or even turning the pages of hard copies of the Reviews (should one be so fortunate as to access them) will not enable modern readers to see the essential minutia of materiality or grasp the breadth of the curated dataset the Reviews bring together.

As this chapter shows, by first recognizing contemporary practices of reading Review periodicals, scholars can follow the ideas and conversations about texts to which Review readers like Hunter were exposed. The chronicle- and catalogue-style reading practices of Review audiences gave them access to the inside jokes, trends, and rhetorics used by these periodicals and enabled them to make connections between authors, publications, publishers, and ideas through those works' cross-connections in the Review database. And so we require access to those Reviews in a curated form with historical and literary context, such as the scholarly edition provides for other works. Exposing these contemporary reading habits adds to our limited knowledge of reading practices in eighteenth-century England, and incorporating such practices into our scholarship of the period using this book's curated dataset will reveal a more robust narrative of criticism and reception—one in which readers situated a specific work amid the conversation Reviews had about genre, canon formation, and the state of English print publication across the eighteenth and early nineteenth century. It will also help us build better digital tools with which we can preserve and study periodicals—their production, their authors, their circulation, and their readers.

CHAPTER TWO

A Dialogue in Print

Reviews and Novel Prefaces

Readers turning to the Monthly Catalogue of the February 1790 issue of the *Monthly Review* would have encountered, immediately under the "Novels" heading, a review for Regina Maria Roche's *The Vicar of Lansdowne; or Country Quarters. A Tale* (1789).[1] The review stands out in this section for its length—it is about a page long. Reviews of novels in the Monthly Catalogue from this period usually averaged less than half a page.[2] Spanning the bottom verso on page 222 and the top three-quarters of the recto page 223, the uncanny length of this Monthly Catalogue review would immediately strike a reader spreading open the periodical before them (Fig. 2.1a and 2.1b). Its length is not all that stands out about this notice of Roche's novel. After complimenting her as "greatly superior to the *mob of novelists who write with ease*" (emphasis original), the review includes a series of short positive statements about the content of Roche's work.[3] It is a "plain and simple tale" that "has contrived to interest us sufficiently."[4] These statements reflect the common makeup of a lukewarm but not defamatory novel review. The next quarter of a page is taken up with the author's preface in its entirety, reflecting a departure from the regular practice of providing quotes in the front section of the Review, and then only to show examples of the author's writing to corroborate the review's evaluation.[5] This reprinting of Roche's preface that breaks with multiple Monthly Catalogue novel-reviewing traditions draws the reader's attention away from the story in Roche's novel and toward the "*saucy humility*" (emphasis original) she used to address the critics.[6]

After her self-published debut with *The Vicar of Lansdowne*, Roche went on to author at least 19 other novels in her 30-year career, publishing largely with William Lane's Minerva Press. Her works went into multiple editions and were also published in Irish and American imprints. She was a prolific novel writer, and her novels were popular. At the outset of her career, when the Review reprinted her first preface in their pages, they invited England's reading public to, without rushing out to purchase the novel, witness a dialogue between the Reviews and a woman novelist across the boundaries of their respective print pages. As readers could see in the review, the novice Roche "invoke[s] not you, ye TUNEFUL NINE," but rather an earthlier tribunal: "To you, O YE CRIT-ICS! I address my fervent prayer; and I implore you to disregard this humble TALE."[7] Roche knew that reviewers of the novel published "cruelly crush[ing]" and "stifl[ing]" criticisms of the genre.[8] She had clearly been paying attention to reviews of novels before she published her own.

The *Monthly Review* identified itself as one of Roche's critics when it re-sponded directly to her preface and quoted it at length. By comparing the Re-views to the Muses, Roche is acknowledging them as purveyors of literary taste. While the Muses would elevate her writing, however, the Reviews would surely damn it. She therefore "entreats" the critics to neglect it, to let it "pass by in unheeded insignificance and reserve your sagacious animadversions" for more "stupendous works."[9] Her novel "cannot be worthy of your high attention," she claims, using humility and flattery to appeal to the Reviews for leniency.[10] Fa-miliar with Review criticisms of the novel, Roche appears to address the peri-odicals in her preface to forestall or avoid criticism. Before printing her preface, the *Monthly* states bluntly: "Her novel is far from being faultless in point of composition; and her *saucy humility* had better have been spared." It is odd, then, that the Reviews reprint the very "*saucy*" words that they suggest Roche never should have written.

The *Critical Review* also responds to Roche's prefatory plea, though not so extensively. In their June 1789 Monthly Catalogue review, the *Critical* gives the novel half a page's attention (though no excerpt), stating that they will not grant "the author's request," which "deviate[s] so far from the usual desire of being noticed, except she feared that our attention would be followed by dislike."[11] The *Critical*'s answer to her preface and the *Monthly*'s reprinting of Roche's address to the Reviews, however, not only expose this back-and-forth between

Council's Report, part iv. No. 17 and 18, gives three different estimates:

    ' 1. By Mr. Chalmers,   -   -   £. 36,810,305

    ' 2. One, seemingly by the privy council itself, 64,668,658

    ' 3. One by the merchants and planters, - 70,000,000

' The argument stands nearly the same, there being as little likelihood that parliament will indemnify the planters for 36,810,395l. as for 70,000,000l. But it is a gross inaccuracy, and the note is not impertinent.'

We understand that the author of the " *Doubts*, &c." is John Ranby, Esq. a gentleman formerly at the Bar.

Art. 22. *Observations on the true Methods of Treatment and Usage of the Negroe Slaves* in the British West India Islands. And a Refutation of the gross Misrepresentations calculated to impose on the Nation, on that Subject. By Thomas Atwood. 8vo. pp. 15. 1s. Mott, in Nagg's Head Court, Grace Church-street.

Mr. A. earnestly contends, in this small and ill-written pamphlet, that the state of the negroe slaves in our West Indies is highly preferable to that of their countrymen who remain in their native African soil, under the cruel dominion of the worst of despots. He tells us, that he was, for twenty-one years, an eye-witness of the manner in which the blacks are, generally, with scarce any exception, treated by their masters, the West India planters ; and he scruples not to declare his preference of their condition to that of the poor labourers in England.—As we cannot pretend to controvert matters of fact, which, he avers, passed under his own actual observation, neither can we afford the most unreserved credit to the representations of a person who manifests so little candour of disposition, as to describe the advocates for the abolition of slavery, as ' a set of men who, under the appearance of being actuated by motives of humanity, are industriously endeavouring to ruin the English West India islands, and contriving to lessen the importance of those settlements to Great Britain.'—Surely this indiscriminate censure argues great ignorance of the characters of many of the *persons* here pointed at, or a *want* of impartiality, which is a thousand times more blameable than mere ignorance ! Mr. Atwood's ill writing may be excused : but bad language, *bad* in every sense of the words, is intolerable !

NOVELS.

Art. 23. *The Vicar of Lansdowne* ; or Country Quarters. A Tale. By Maria Regina Dalton. 12mo. 2 Vols. 6s. sewed. Johnson. 1789.

This authoress is greatly superior to the *mob of novelists who write with ease* :—(For that performances of the present kind are *easily written*, we may fairly conclude, from the very great number which are continually presented to us.)—She aims, occasionally, at a display of *character* ; and not unfrequently delineates it with tolerable success. This, as we have repeatedly observed, is the principal excellence in a novel, as it is in a dramatic production. Miss Dalton too, in a plain and simple tale (which we would always prefer to that which is complex, because the figures may

con-

Figure 2.1a, 2.1b. (*above and opposite*) *The Monthly Review*'s review of Regina Maria Roche's *The Vicar of Lansdowne*, 2nd ser., 1 (February 1790): 222–223. Copy held by Princeton University.

confequently be drawn with a bolder hand) has contrived to interest us fufficiently in the event. Attention is kept awake, while the fentiments are fuch as every good and fufceptible heart muft thoroughly approve.

As this writer will probably appear again before the tribunal of the public, we are induced to prefent her with a word of advice, viz. " *to admire fuperior fenfe and doubt her own.*" The following quotation from the preface to this work, will fhew that fhe does not deem too humbly of her own abilities. Her novel is far from being faultlefs in point of compofition; and her *faucy humility* had better have been fpared.

' To you, O ye critics! I addrefs my fervent prayer; and I implore you to difregard this humble Tale. The amufement of a few folitary hours cannot be worthy of your high attention. Unftudied, unornamented as it is, it may, perhaps, beguile fome tedious interval, if your cenfures do not cruelly crufh the flattering hope, and ftifle my poor bantling on its firft ftruggles into life. Permit it, I entreat you, to pafs by in unheeded infignificance, and referve your fagacious animadverfions for thofe ftupendous works, that, like the pyramids of Egypt, rife fucceffively above each other, and provoke, by their pretenfions to fame, an inquiry into the nature of their ftructure, and the bafis of their elevation.'

Having hinted at fome errors in this production, we had, at firft, an intention of pointing them out. Its general merit, however, is fo confiderable, that we have dropped that defign.—For, to talk in the quaint kind of language of the authorefs, ' *a fhort time produced reciprocal dilection in our bofoms, indicative of the pureft friendfhip.*'—A friendfhip, by the way, which we fhall willingly cultivate, *if to this lady it may feem good.*

Art. 24. *Darnley Vale*; or Emelia Fitzroy. By Mrs. Bonhote *.
12mo. 3 Vols. 7s. 6d. fewed. Lane. 1789.

The main object of this performance is to prove, that a woman, when difappointed in a *firft* attachment of the heart, may be perfectly happy in a *fecond*. This is exemplified in the hiftory of Emelia Fitzroy. Being deferted by Mr. Vernon, to whom her affections had long been given, fhe is afterward married to Lord Eltham, a nobleman of the moft amiable and engaging manners: while her quondam admirer, having, " like the bafe Indian, thrown a pearl away richer than all his tribe,"—is (we fuppofe to punifh him for his *apoftacy*) wedded to a downright virago; in whofe fociety, he experiences every mifery which the married ftate affords when the connexion has been improperly formed. With regard to the other characters, they are of the ordinary fize and quality; and, like the walking ladies and gentlemen of the ftage, ferve to fill up the fcene without having any material bufinefs in the piece. The volumes are pleafingly, and, with fome few exceptions, very correctly written; and the leffons in virtue and morality do the greateft honour to the writer's heart. A beautiful

---

* For this Lady's " Parental Monitor," fee Rev. vol. lxxix. p. 173.

picture

themselves and the novelist to their readers; they also mark Roche's preface, and therefore Roche herself, as somehow worthy of entering into conversation with in the first place, despite their criticisms of her.

Roche was not alone in addressing the Reviews in her prefatory material. The performances of humility, pleas for fair treatment, entreaties for leniency, and explanations for errors in women's novel prefaces during the Romantic period, or rather, the Minerva Era, in response to book reviews draw scholars to the tension between these writers and the reviewing system.[12] Specifically, since novel reviews were themselves particularly gendered pieces of writing, this tension is notable when it comes to how women writers responded to them and how the male-coded reviews answered back.[13] The criticisms in book reviews often served as catalysts for the forestalling words that women novelists used to precede their works of imagination and the ways they worked to shape that genre in response.[14] While we should be wary of conflating these women writers' authorial personas with their actual identities, these prefaces provide a glimpse into their knowledgeable and vehement engagement in a literary system that pressed on and circulated expectations for the genre they were actively shaping. For the most part, no other body of these women's own words about their writing or their role in the book market survives, and *this* body of writing is readily available—not scattered in manuscripts or letters, but in print—at the beginning of every book.

In this chapter, I argue that the reprinting of these prefaces and the ways the reviewing system responds to them within *their* pages, when studied en masse for the first time, illuminate a different reading of these novel prefaces than we have heretofore been able to access. Aligning with Jennie Batchelor's establishment of authors of *The Lady's Magazine* and the journal itself as decidedly "unRomantic," the dialogue I uncover also "fail[s] to subscribe to the conventional hierarchies of authorship, genius, gender and genre that were formalized in the Romantic period itself," in part by pushing back against the Enlightenment definitions of professional authorship that already haunted women writers.[15] Batchelor's survey of women writers' applications to the Royal Literary Fund reveals that these authors used their prefaces to write against the conceptions of feminine authorship that the Fund, aligning with Review criticism of the day, pitted against professional authorship. The Fund and the Reviews were focused on "genius" authors and "men of letters," where "genius was defined in opposition to domestic life" and the writing of women.

Building on Batchelor's insight that points to the domestic positioning of these women's prefaces as "particularly effective weapons in a woman writer's arsenal," I argue that reading these prefaces anew in light of Review responses to them within the literary system of reviewing illuminates this dialogue as far more nuanced and powerful on the part of women writers than simple authorial pleas meeting literary criticism.[16] "Not every Romantic-era woman writer," Pam Perkins writes in her study of Anne Grant and Elizabeth Hamilton, "was destined to be a hapless victim of critical violence or a passive object inscribed within a narrowly prescriptive and trivialized version of literary femininity."[17] And indeed, by proposing a taxonomy for women novelists' prefaces from this period and reading them together with the Review responses to them, I show that these women novelists were in fact *shaping* the criticism flung against them. Together, these prefaces do parallel work to what Hannah Doherty Hudson shows the volume of novels could do and what Elizabeth Neiman shows that the repetition in those novels' stories did—"collectively recirculate, engage and modify commonplaces about women's nature, the social order . . . and Romantic redefinitions of authorship and literature."[18]

Using 350 novel prefaces by women and anonymous novelists from the *NRD*, I identify eight prefatory traditions from this period. Categorizing how these traditions interact with Review criticism, I map how the Reviews themselves respond to these prefaces, even when they seem aware that writers are using the prefaces to goad them into a response. Reading prefaces and parody prefaces within the context of Review responses, I show that during this period, women novelists' paratexts cannibalized the very pages that set out to criticize, instruct, harangue, or generally control *them* and their chosen genre. This helps us think about these novelists as not just shaping genre but also as (whether to their detriment or not) having a hand in puppeteering the reviews they received. Even if they did not receive favorable feedback, what they emphasized in their prefaces could steer a review through detailed stories, misdirection, or feigned fragility.

Definitions of feminine authorship were a major point of discussion in reviews of Romantic-era novels.[19] I show here that these exchanges in the Reviews were often driven or instigated by women novelists themselves. At times, these women novelists were able to infuse their own voices into the Reviews' pages, and in doing so, they brought conversations about genre boundaries and gendered authorship out of high-literary debates and into the general public's eye. If we think of reading reviews and novels (and their prefaces) en masse the way a voracious contemporary novel reader or even a reader interested in genre policing might have, we can see that the debate is not top-down with the Reviews in control, nor is it individual authors simpering back to the Reviews in their prefaces. Read together, these prefaces elevate their authors' desired topics of discussion and force the Reviews to out their own anxieties about authorship and genre.

Listening to the Data

I compiled this catalogue of reviews engaging with novel prefaces by women or anonymous authors when building the *NRD*. While systematically reading 1,636 book reviews, I noticed a pattern of reviews quoting from novels' prefaces rather than from the body of the work.[20] Kandice Sharren calls this type of discovery "data intimacy"—the act of intuiting and noticing connections and threads in our data because of the time we spend with it and not necessarily because of the computational queries we run upon it.[21] The intimacy garnered by the practice of chronicle-style reading of the Reviews would also highlight these conversations for contemporaries. Herein I focus on prefatory exchanges between women and anonymous novelists and the Reviews. I do so not because male novelists did *not* participate in such exchanges, but rather because attending to the ways that women used this space and opportunity for dialogue offers a new reading of the gendered reviewing of the English novel when women were dominantly authoring it. The way that relationship plays out is surprising.

From 1790 to 1820, the *Monthly* and the *Critical Review* published several reviews that addressed novels' prefatory material. The exchanges I trace in this chapter highlight how both sides of this cross-print dialogue leaned heavily on the authors' gender (or assumed feminine gender for anonymously published works, as was often the case in reviews) as central to their understanding of and arguments concerning authorship, style, criticism, experience, expertise, and genre boundaries. The Reviews' direct references to prefaces are often in the form of citations to the prefatory material as catalysts for including certain review content. These direct references range from quoting, paraphrasing, or explicit replies (e.g., "in response to the authoress's question"). The number of reviews' responses is in fact far greater when considering indirect references, which may have been obscured to contemporary (and certainly to modern) Review readers if they did not have access to the novel in question.

Review rhetoric would have contemporary readers and modern scholars alike believing that their primary role was to admonish feminine novelists. But their overwhelming interaction with these writers *on those writers' own terms* tells another story. Of the 350 reviews tracked in this chapter that somehow engage with novel paratext, 161 feature direct references to the novel's preface in their review. Considering the number of now-identified women novelists herein (241), that means that 69 percent of these reviews' direct references to prefaces are to works that we now *know* were authored by women. The percentage of review responses to women novelists is likely greater when taking into account the reviews of novels whose authorial gender is still unknown, which Garside and Raven suggest is about 80 percent of anonymously published novels from this period.[22] This would mean that about 94 percent of the reviews in this study that spoke to the prefaces of novels that claimed feminine or anonymous authorship were in fact directly responding to women.

It is meaningful that these reviews interacted so overwhelmingly with the personal or intellectual remarks of feminine novelists, considering that these male reviewers, drawing on eighteenth- and nineteenth-century gender roles and expectations, believed it their duty to guide (and constrain) the genre produced overwhelmingly by women.[23] Women novelists anticipated such policing, stepping outside the pages of their fiction and using their prefaces to beg for pity, challenge Review authority, mock Review criticisms, or draw readers into the argument. And while male novelists also interacted with the Reviews, women writers had fewer opportunities to enter their voice into a public space and had a far shorter tradition and less power to disagree with men in the positions of authority that the Reviews held. I pursue this study of women's prefaces and Review reactions to them not because women acted differently than men—we can and should study gender for more than differences. Rather, I study them here because these women *did* enter into and often drove the conversation, and gender inherently influenced and placed restraints on how and why they did so. "If reviews outline the parameters of this debate," Hudson concludes about the discussion of genre during the Minerva Era, "then new scholarship continues to deepen our understanding of the ways that women writers internalized—and resisted—its terms."[24] In this chapter, I map the dialogue between these masculine reviewers and women novelists, showing the latter as active agents in forecasting the novel's genre boundaries and reception as a respectable form of literature. I also reveal these oft-castigated women writers as themselves autonomous constructors of the content of the reviews through tropes that we might consider criticism baiting.

The dialogue across textual borders between novel prefaces and reviews requires that both genres abandon their previous traditional foci. Generally, we expect reviews to be self-contained, referencing only literary elements of the work being discussed. Prefaces to earlier eighteenth-century novels were self-contained in that they taught readers what to expect in the ensuing text; the prefaces to Daniel Defoe's *Robinson Crusoe* (1719) or Samuel Richardson's *Clarissa* (1747), for example, tell what the stories will entail, entice interest, and instruct the reader how to read them.[25] These novels that predated the establishment of book-reviewing periodicals deployed their prefaces largely to interact with readers. Joseph F. Bartolomeo identifies in women novelists' prefaces across the eighteenth century a search for connection with their readers and an avoidance of drawing attention to their gender as a method for keeping readers focused on their work.[26] In novels by women during the period of this study, however, preparing the general reader for what they are about to encounter is overwhelmingly *not* the preface's focus, and as a result, the Reviews also had a hard time keeping to their own pages. Gerard Genette's formative theory on paratexts refers to them as *seulis*, or thresholds, with an "inward side (turned toward the text) and an outward side (turned toward the world's discourse about the text)."[27] My findings show that women's novel prefaces served as just such a threshold, bowing to both directions. As Hudson shows for Minerva Press authors, however, "given the [novel] prefaces' mediating function, it should not surprise us that they often engage directly with their era's discourse of ever-increasing fictional production." They frequently "echo reviewers" in their anxieties about genre boundaries and reception.[28] But we ought to expand this understanding as going both ways: The reviews echo the novelists as well.

Striking Up a Conversation

By the 1790s, the novel's preface had become a genre of its own and was expected to include certain foundational elements. The prefaces of 350 novels by women reviewed from 1790 to 1820 included specific components that reflect a larger trend toward engagement with the Reviews.[29] Eight conventions emerge when reading all of these prefaces together. While an inward look toward the story was not abandoned by novelists, by 1790, novel prefaces overwhelmingly looked outward, with a specific eye toward the Reviews' critical discourse about the work (Table 2.1). Seven of these eight conventions involve looking outward, whether through direct references to expected Review criticism or by indirectly noting an intention for writing inspired by the need to correct public vices (rather than from a vanity of desired authorship). Five of the prefatory elements (anticipation of criticism, requesting leniency of the critics, mention of the author's experience, references to prefatory elements, and mention of the author's age) are specifically geared away from explaining the novel's contents and instead engage with criticisms of the genre that are specific to the Reviews. An overwhelming 84 percent of prefaces include an anticipation of criticism; it is

| Prefatory Element | Look Outward | | | | | Look Inward | | |
| | Engage with Review Criticism | | | | | | | |
	Anticipate Criticism	Request Leniency of Critics	Mention Author's Experience	Reference Prefatory Elements	Mention Author's Age	Discuss Genre Conventions	Express Intention for Writing	Explain Plot
Of 350 Prefaces	295 84%	204 58%	186 53%	52 15%	47 13%	197 56%	273 78%	36 10%

the *most* common prefatory convention. This marks a new focus for the novel's preface by the 1790s: engaging with criticism.

As Table 2.1 shows, other elements of the novel's preface during this period look to the specific criticisms the Reviews directed at novelists while also highlighting what was to come in the ensuing work. The Reviews defined for the reading public what made a good novel: original plots and stories, well-composed writing, adherence to proper language and grammatical conventions, clear moral lessons, and no vulgarities. Women novelists, with their poor and inconsistent access to education, were the leading victims of these criticisms. The preface conventions of "intention for writing" and "discussion of genre" look inward to the novel itself but also outward to address critical issues the Reviews raised concerning expectations about the novel and its readers. Only the "explanation of plot" convention found in prefaces from this period faces solely toward the inside of the text. That almost all of women novelist's' prefaces during this period include an anticipation of criticism strikingly emphasizes the preface as the place where a dialogue between authors and the Reviews took place.

While some prefaces include only a few of the foundational elements outlined here, Anna Maria Porter's breakout novel, *Artless Tales* (1793), features an archetypal preface, and an examination of it helps us see how it is deployed by authors and what reactions they receive from the Reviews. Porter's preface includes the first four conventions from Table 2.1 that specifically speak to the Reviews: an anticipation of criticism, a request for leniency by the critics, and mention of the author's age and experience. Porter begins by stating that only by the "liberal encouragement" and "kind indulgence" of her friends was she "induced" to publishing. She admits that her "volume will, doubtless, be foun[d to have] many faults" that have "crept in" but notes she should be forgiven for them because of her "youth and inexperience," —she claims to have written the book at the tender age of 13.[30] It may appear that Porter is simply preparing the reader for the whimsical, juvenile stories they are about to encounter. Because prefaces in general are revised or removed across subsequent editions of each novel, their contextuality often makes their meaning elusive for modern readers. Once it is placed in the context of the established cross-genre dialogue, however, we can understand Porter's carefully crafted preface as anticipating and engaging with the criticism that her novel will receive from the Reviews.

When Porter addresses issues in her work that might be found faulty as she "bring[s] it before the eye of the Public," "Public" here is signaling a formal voice of readers, specifically the Reviews, in anticipation of their judgment.[31]

Moving from her expectation of criticism, she requests leniency when wishing her readers would "kindly excuse some inaccuracies" within her novel.[32] Here Porter indicates an expectation that said "inaccuracies" will be used by the Reviews as ammunition to denounce her work. Many novice writers hoped to appeal to the sympathy of the Reviews and avoid such slights by noting their "youth and inexperience."[33] This could, as Porter requests, excuse any errors in writing, plot, or unwise decisions to publish. These age-related references were appeals for forgiving reviews, like those of 17-year-old Margaret Holford's novel *Calaf; a Persian Tale* (1799). Of this work, the *Critical* stated: "From that age it would be unreasonable to expect much; yet there is a promise of improvement, which we would wish to encourage."[34] The *Monthly* was similarly merciful in reaction to Holford: "We throw aside the pen of criticism; recollecting, as we do, (with not over-fond remembrance,) that we too have been young writers."[35] A preface's inclusion of the inexperienced author's age could also result in a more chiding response, such as the *Critical*'s 1800 review of young Anne Kerr's *Adeline St. Julian* (1800), which states: "Deprecating, as we do, such a prostitution of the press, we advise this lady to relinquish the employment of writing for the public."[36] The possibility of such widely ranging responses explains Porter's inclusion of her extremely tender age of 13 in her preface—and why her mention of this fact was deceptive. Born on December 22, 1778, Porter was actually 15 at the time of *Artless Tales*'s publication, though she may have indeed been 13 when she wrote it. Regardless, her attempt to cloud her age and experience speaks to her familiarity with Review practices, and her preface shows an effort to manipulate their criticisms.[37]

The prefatory conventions that Porter deploys are themselves a catalyst for a dialogue in print across two genres and between two groups who regularly declared themselves opposites. As responses *to* commonly known Review criticisms, these women's prefaces are a *reply* to the decades of critique these "grey beards" (as they call themselves in response to another preface) had regularly slung at the novel and especially at its feminine authorship.[38] A *reply* here is different from a *reaction*. Rather than thinking of these prefatory conventions used by women writers as only a defense (reaction), we might consider them as the initiation (reply, catalyst) of a dialogue. They disrupt the reviewing system's assumption that it is the only or dominant voice where subjects of authorship and genre are concerned and counter the Reviews' attitude in their criticisms, which projected a top-down lecture format. Similar to how the subscribers of *The Lady's Magazine* had a hand in the journal, these novelists "imagined themselves to be active participants in the [periodical's] print community, which gave them an opportunity to participate in an ongoing and widespread conversation about the world and women's place within it."[39]

These prefaces might be viewed as women writers walking onto the stage of debate and discussion about their authorship and the novel's development. Porter's reply to popular Review criticisms via her preface shows that novelists were aware of such dialogue and were familiar with how generic foundations of the preface enabled them to participate in it. Even as a young first-time novelist, Porter was well versed enough to join in. It is not until the Reviews respond to these prefaces, though, that we might fully name this a dialogue. While the Reviews' initial criticisms of novels may have (in their minds) been statements, women novelists' prefaces open the door to an opportunity for it to be a *conversation*—but only if the Reviews keep talking. Amid all their power and insistence on being the sole voice of reason, it is the Reviews' response to those prefaces that provides the means for a dialogue to progress wherein women novelists make up half of the voices.

We can now read Porter's preface as the second voice in this conversation, responding to Review critiques with formulated conventions and expecting, or instigating, a reply in-kind from the Reviews. And it works. In September 1793, the *Critical Review* answers, stating: "These Tales, the author tells us, were written at the age of thirteen, and we readily believe it, as they bear the marks of that sweet delirium, into which the young mind is apt to be plunged." They forgive her youth to some degree and offer her a two-page review in the front of the periodical rather than consigning her to the Monthly Catalogue. One page of this review is a complimentary excerpt from *Artless Tales*, but almost the entirety of the page of critical discussion is an interaction with her preface and the title of her work. The reviewer comments on her professed age, rails against her title, and touches on the story of her friends encouraging her to publish. Overwhelmingly, it is Porter's preface that guides the content of her review.[40] The giants of literary criticism bring very little insight or critique to their article that Porter had not already touched on herself. This is not the only time an author's preface clearly guided the content of their review. In one extreme example, half of the two-sentence review of Anna Thomson's *The Duchess of York, an English Story* (1791) reads simply: "What can we say? The preface disarms criticism."[41] Though relying on their same tired rubric for evaluating novels often resulted in formulaic reviews, these periodicals could not help themselves but to speak to novelists' prefatory content.[42]

When book reviews respond to novelists' prefaces and enter a dialogue about the genre with that author, they also invite Review readers to listen in. There is an abundance of review–preface dialogue that is difficult to access when reading only one of the texts at hand, and even having read both genres is not enough. A working knowledge of prefaces and of book reviewing does not raise this dialogue to the forefront. This is because nearly 50 percent of the review responses to prefaces are unremarkable to the general reader. They respond to the content of the author's preface without drawing attention to the fact that they are doing so. But for the other half of review responses, there are plentiful markers that indicate to the reader that a back-and-forth has ensued. Phrases like "In the preface," "we are told in the preface," "the following passage in her Introduction," "the author says," "the author requests," "in the introduction," "says the advertisement," "we turn back to her preface," and "as the writer informs us" serve as signals to Review readers that they have come in after the dialogue has already begun. These readers, then, have every enticement to peek into these novels, seeking out those prefaces to see just what each review is responding to.

Readers may also have merely speculated about what the authors were saying in their prefaces based on context clues in the reviews. The Reviews' use of these markers is surprising in that they voluntarily make this conversation visible. Whereas the Reviews can and do converse across textual borders with these novelists in ways that do not draw attention to that dialogue, and despite their regularly and vehemently insisting on their superiority over novel writers, at times they seem to want to show themselves as talking with or chiding these authors. This is all the more striking for women novelists, as these conversations often press on what professional authorship, and feminine authorship in particular, was and ought to be. The Reviews could slide their admonishments or responses under the radar of general readers but either decide instead to bring it forward to the public or are goaded into it by the authors themselves.

We might begin to think of the content of reviews not just as criticism that the reviewers slung at authors but as topics related to genre development, professional authorship, or story that the authors themselves found valuable and instigated conversation about. How, for example, do the *Monthly*'s reviewers of Mary Hays's *Memoirs of Emma Courtney* (1796) know that "the fair writer aims at the solution of a moral problem which is eminently important" without her preface telling them? Discussion of this "moral problem" and how her novel tackles it makes up the entirety of the review's criticism. The reviewers even close by stating: "We refrain from minute criticisms on plot, incident, or character, in a work which is marked by such uncommon features as those which characterise the present volumes."[43] Hays's preface amounted to a misdirection of their petty criticisms and kept their focus on the larger issues she was exploring in her fiction. The entire content of the *Monthly*'s review of *The Lake of Killarney* (1804) is a reaction to its preface, which stated that the author (Porter again) was unwell when she wrote it and that she intended it for amusement rather than instruction.[44] In another example of review content prompted by paratext, the *Critical* is enticed into answering to "the introduction of this work," *Bungay Castle* (1797), because the author "professes 'to consider the reviewers as friends,'" quoting Elizabeth Bonhonte's coy flattery before offering a critique on her story.[45]

When women novelists did not draw the Reviews into conversation through misleading or evasive prefaces, their textual presence *as women* drew Review attention. The textual repurposing of prefaces for Review content highlights Review anxiety that the voices of women novelists would or could take up space in the discussion about authorship and genre. This anxiety culminates in one of the Review's criticisms of this prefatory material: an insistence that the person of the novelist should not be present in the text. This is not a criticism that the Reviews articulate in response to masculine novelists nor one that we see when the work under review has no prefatory material. But the body of women's fiction and the prefaces themselves are on the receiving end of this flavor of judgment. The *Monthly* expresses its concern with *The History of Netterville, a chance Pedestrian* (1802), noting, "We observe that this lady introduces *herself* not unfrequently" and insisting "the author should be so far in the back ground [*sic*], as neither to think nor hear *in propriâ personâ*."[46]

Reviewers remind readers of this expectation of a novelist's invisibility when remarking that outcries against Anna Maria Bennett's *Agnes de Courci, a tale* (1789) "seem to have forgotten that the *author* of a novel, as of a drama, never speaks; and that it is only with a view to preserve the truth of the representation, when any thing [*sic*] censurable is put into the mouths of his actors."[47] The *Critical* takes issue with Emma Parker putting herself forward by expounding in her preface of *Aretas, a Novel* (1813) about the labor of writing and entreats her to silence: "If Miss Parker is so well aware of the difficulties of novel writing as she pretends, we would advise her for the future not to *talk so much about it*; but to set to work in right earnest."[48] Their saltiness and hope to quiet Parker may come from her preface's jab that, as opposed to novels, "periodical papers . . . appear to me to be the most easy and agreeable, of all descriptions of writing; while as much or as little as is convenient may be said."[49] Parker had already received censure by the Reviews a year before for including in *Virginia; or, the*

Peace of Amiens (1811) not only a preface that professed her thoughts on writing but also what she called "preludes" to each volume, where she outlined her decision-making process in crafting the story "following, in some measure, the example of Fielding."[50] "How far is this delving system likely to succeed?" the *Critical* responds, exasperated, advising her "to think with more diffidence of [her] own abilities."[51] Though the reviewers were drawn into conversation with these novelists by their prefaces and often knew the authors' gender (their regular admonishment of "the fair authoress" makes this unmistakable), it seems that the pointed reminder of the existence of real women writing the pages they read was an anathema for the Reviews and another way that the novelists could draw them into conversation.

The makeup of these reviews, which are written in response to the prefaces, is therefore effectively manufactured by the novelists themselves. This is epitomized by reviews quoting extensively from the authors' prefaces rather than from their novels, as we saw with Roche's *Vicar of Lansdowne*. Such quoting is a constant practice across the period. The review of Jane West's *The Loyalists; an historical novel* (1812) includes five excerpts from the text, one a paragraph from her introductory chapter that lays out "her motives for writing the present historical novel." Commentary on those motives make up one page of the two and one-quarter pages of criticism she receives in addition to the excerpts.[52] Almost half of the discussion of West's novel in the review pages is focused on and directed by her own remarks. One-third of the review of Rachel Hunter's *Letters from Mrs. Palmerstone to her Daughter* (1804) is a paratext quote, and the *Monthly*'s notice of Caroline Richardson's *Adonia, a desultory Story* (1801) quotes two paragraphs from her preface, taking up a full page and leaving only one-quarter page for the reviewer's own voice.[53] The review for *Ulric and Ilvina: the Scandinavian Tale* (1797), a novel whose authorship is still unknown but claims a feminine hand of only "eighteen suns" (18 years old), reprints ten lines of the work's poetical preface.[54] These reviews are directed in subject matter by the prefaces *and* are made up of the novelists' own words, sometimes to the degree that the author's voice overshadows that of the critic.

These are moments when the Reviews, even in their criticism, fall into a common periodical practice: reprinting other work to fill their pages. This was, of course, the model that many periodicals used and that readers would not be surprised to find. The novelists' prefaces succeed in drawing the Reviews into a print conversation, however, and the Reviews in turn make that conversation visible and accessible to *their* readers by marking their replies and reprinting the paratext they are replying to. By reprinting paratextual material in place of stylistic excerpts or their own critical voices, the Reviews effectively encourage authors to read one another's prefaces as well, helping to aid in the construction of preface conventions and build a network of voices capable of upholding a dialogue with the large, advanced, established, and widely circulating reviewing system. The very men who set out to police and control women novelists in fact built them a platform from which to speak.

Parody Prefaces

The Reviews continue the tradition of this dialogue when the *Critical* devotes one-quarter of a page to quoting from the preface of Sarah Green's *Romance Readers and Romance Writers, a Satirical Novel* (1810).[55] The title of this novel draws attention to its satirical form and content, and the story follows a quixotic young woman and her comical misguided adventures as she attempts to apply the fantastical lessons from her novel reading to her real life. Green's preface to this gothic novel parody is also itself a parody; in it, she jokes about the over-the-top claims of found manuscripts and speaks back to the preface's textual claims in her footnotes.[56] The *Critical* flollows Green's satirical play with gothic novel tropes, calling attention to her preface in their review. Green's humor depends on criticizing novels, and so the Reviews join in. The *Critical*'s interaction with Green regarding a satire of the novel stands in stark contrast to their silence in reaction to parody prefaces whose focus is to critique the degree to which the aforementioned preface categories cajole, appease, or pander to the Reviews' power and perspectives. Though I have established that the Reviews are guided by these prefaces, they still seem to feel that they have the upper hand. Parody prefaces, on the other hand, remind the Reviews that women writers have enough smarts and agency to identify the pitfalls and hypocrisies of the reviewing system.

Novels throughout the eighteenth century used parody to, as April London puts it, "contemplate [their] own evolving literary history," and the parody preface was no different.[57] Perhaps the most famous of the genre, Laurence Sterne's parody preface in the notoriously self-aware novel *Tristram Shandy* (1759–1767), does not appear until volume three, and in typical Shandean fashion, it never quite gets to the point.[58] Parodic prefaces during the Minerva Era pronounce the commonality of the preface–Review conversation by staging ridiculous recitals of the expectations of that dialogue. *The Advertisement* (1818), by Elizabeth Clark for example, is a novel whose very title is another moniker used for prefatory paratext. Its parodic preface begins with a falsified exclamation: *"A Preface!"* (italics original). The reader (and reviewer) is forced to exclaim along with Clark at the preface's appearance, dramatizing its existence and function. *Why is the preface there?* the author pretends to wonder in the ensuing paragraphs: "Is it in order to deprecate the severity of that lash, which snarling would-be critics are always ready to inflict?" "No; for such I care not," she insists. Her two-page parody preface focuses specifically on the prefatory habit of groveling to the Reviews. References to the "snarling" Reviews' "lash" are reminiscent of Roche's prefatory fear that they would "cruelly crush" her novel.[59] Clark's preface tells us what the author will *not* do by offering a dramatic parody against traditional preface–Review exchange elements. She will not "confess the reasons which induced [her] to stand forth a candidate for public favour" or "crave the mercy and indulgence of [her] readers toward her humble performance." Indeed, on whether to include each prefatory convention, Clark responds theatrically: "I answer *no!*"[60]

Yet without the recitation of these included elements in a traditional form, Clark does not receive a Review response to her preface. The *Monthly*'s one-third page of attention in the Monthly Catalogue blandly notes that the novel "contains even more egregious improbabilities" than generally observed "in similar productions" and then proceeds to list examples of her "incorrect and affected jargon."[61] Clark's preface is not mentioned directly nor interacted with indirectly. Though the inclusion of the charted prefatory elements often drove review content, when bandied by an authoress like Clark in criticism of the Reviews themselves, they are ignored by those stalwart gentlemen, who refuse to interact.

The same can be seen in the Reviews' lack of response to *Something Odd!* (1804) by Elizabeth Meeke. The novel includes a parodic preface entitled "A Dialogue Between The Author and His Pen," wherein the author's pen is anthropomorphized to ask about their intention to include each formulaic prefatory convention. Looking upon the writer, the pen declares: "You are conning something in the way of preface, advertisement, introduction, some mode of opening, of entrance to the little fabric you have raised." The pen then asks if the author will include several traditional prefatorial elements—a motive for writing, a dedication, an insistence that the story is "founded upon facts."[62] The pen asks at last, "What do you think those formidable beings, the critics, will say to your book?" The author offers a burlesque response: "I answer that, in trembling humility (for a quivering fit has at last come upon me), I throw myself upon their mercy, and hope—Oh! I hope for a favourable fait!"[63] The review of *Something Odd* in the *Critical* is terse; only five sentences, it takes up a mere quarter of a page.[64] Meeke's preface is not mentioned at all. This lack of response is most striking when we consider that Meeke is the stepsister of Frances Burney, whose dialogue with the Reviews from the preface of *Evelina* (1778), which announces itself as addressed "to the Authors of the Monthly and Critical Reviews" and which opened this book, is the most documented example of this conversation.[65]

If the Reviews' engagement with or reprinting of prefatorial content made the dialogue between novelists and reviewers visible and accessible to Review readers, then this lack of response suggests an attempt to hide the parody preface's jabs. The Reviews cannot even be tempted by the parody dedication to *The Orientalist: Or, Electioneering in Ireland: A Tale* (1820) by Mrs. Purcell. Four pages of paratext ask repeatedly about suitable candidates for a dedication, and the only conclusion the author meets the queries with is that she will dedicate it to "MYSELF."[66] Such pride and unRomantic authorship flies in the face of the Reviews' insistence on demure intentions for feminine writings, goading the Reviews to reply. But they do not. That the Reviews are indeed being baited by women writers' prefaces is emphasized by their silence when these formulaic pleas and prefatory tropes are called out by a parody preface. In reviews of these novels, the critics stick strictly to their formula, critiquing individuality, probability, plot, and errors in the syntax or style. When the authors draw attention to the formula, the Reviews dig their heels in and pretend not to notice. They give no indication to Review readers that the authors have criticized them.

When we consider that 92 percent of the reviews of these 350 novels interacted with their prefaces, these prefaces might be recognized as not just a responses *to* reviews but as a catalyst *for* the reviews themselves. This makes those novelists effectively the authors of circulating criticism on the genre, hijackers of the reviewing system. While women writers could not, with a single novel or its preface, alter the definitions of professional authorship that the Reviews touted, their prefatorial pages drew Reviewers into a conversation whereby commenting on those prefaces marked women novelists as worthy of engaging with in a public discourse. At the very least, Review responses marked the words women published about their own books as a viable threat to the periodical's own criticisms.

Despite Review clapbacks, novelists continued to write prefaces that called out the common slanders and gatekeeping of the reviewing system. This indicates to us that Review put-downs were not the death blows they were intended to be and were perhaps received by the authors and readers as unnecessarily loud castigations of genre boundaries that did not automatically seep into public consciousness. Reading Review responses to prefaces en masse helps us to critically examine *how* these responses to women writers influence our own scholarship and to what degree the Reviews created an illusion of the period's novel reading and writing marketplace that extended into twentieth-century criticism. While some women novelists may have used the preface as an attempted or postured defense and others considered it an offensive move to push away possible conflict or shape a literary persona, we might also think of these prefaces as a more nuanced combination that resists these oppositional categories. Prefaces were a space where women practiced or performed known expectations for feminine authorship but were also arenas for baiting and agitating the anxieties of the Reviews and even heightening those anxieties as a form of control or autonomy.

In this act of unRomantic authorship, women writers were agents of the Reviews. That these novelists could drive such content highlights how high the Review anxieties were about women's dominance over novel authorship at the time and how they feared they might be losing their firm hold on the reins of literary boundaries. The grey-beard reviewer lecturing the young miss authoress was a caricature they hoped to stress. In actuality, the market was changing right under the Reviews' feet in ways that gave authors more agency, and this was driven by readers and their preferences (as highlighted by Lane's successful circulating libraries) more than ever before. An examination of women novelists' prefaces and how they pull the strings on the reviewing system shows us that the discussion of genre was wrested by its authorship from the reins of literary critics.

CHAPTER THREE

The Rise and Fall of Charlotte Smith, Novelist

In Charlotte Turner Smith's (1749–1806) career as a novelist, she published 46 volumes of fiction, the bulk of them in the 1790s.[1] Smith was one of the most prolific novelists of the period and a celebrated poet; her *Elegiac Sonnets* (1784) went into nine editions during her lifetime. She was also one of the Romantic period's most reviewed women writers.[2] Across her voluminous publications, Smith was known for monopolizing her prefatory material to craft literary personas and appeal to public sentiment to support her image and finances. Despite her financial and domestic hardships, nobody could suggest that Smith had no voice where her experiences, her authorship, or her contributions to discussions of genre were concerned.

Unsurprisingly, the reviewing system had much to say on the many productions of Smith's pen and the content of her not-so-subtle prefatory writings about herself and genre. In 1996, Carrol L. Fry stated, "If Smith had written nothing more than the early novels and the first few editions of *Elegiac Sonnets*, she might justly be remembered as the innovator of an amusing but trivial subgenre of fiction, and a poet with a feel for popular taste. Her later novels, however, are on the cutting edge at a critical moment in history."[3] Fry's words reflect the majority of scholarship concerning Smith's novels across the nineteenth and twentieth centuries. Soon after Smith's death, Anna Laetitia Barbauld included only one of Smith's "early novels" in her *The British Novelists* (1810) collection, and by the time Sir Walter Scott edited the Ballantyne *British Novelists* (1821–1824) collection, she was not included all.[4] Smith was relegated to his "miscellaneous" supplement. It is to this moment that Fry identifies, this division of Smith's career as a novelist between those early and later novels, that this chapter turns to, because understanding Smith's career as a novelist without considering it within the contemporary reviewing system has left scholars today without essential context for her legacy.

In recent years, scholarship on Smith's novels has grown significantly. All of her original novels are now available in scholarly and teaching editions. Research on her characters, her influence on other major novelists, and her fiction as part of larger genre and historical movements has brought Smith back into our conversation about influential novelists from the Romantic period.[5] This is all especially valuable considering that for decades, scholarship on Smith was largely focused on her poetry, since it was as a poet that she was revived to the canon by the 1980s feminist literary recovery movement. Jacqueline Labbe and Stuart Curran established that she was more than Fry's poet with a "feel for popular taste"—she was in fact a great innovator of Romantic poetry and a remarkable example of women's authorship in general.[6] Most recently, Labbe has traced Smith's authorial exchanges with William Wordsworth, showing that she was instrumental in establishing the basis of Romantic poetry's sentimental and experimental nature.[7] Smith studies have also benefitted from new interest in her children's literature and her herbalist and botany publications.[8] At last the great breadth and diversity of Smith's textual oeuvre is receiving the attention it is due.

So much of the current scholarship on Smith, however, grapples with who the "real" Smith might be. For most of Smith's feminine novel-writing contemporaries, there remain only vague historical references and a smattering of biographical details to help us know them beyond their printed words. For Smith, however, we have a vast collection of correspondence made readily available by years of painstaking collecting and editing by Judith Stanton.[9] Smith's letters reveal an astute author who crafted her fiction with intelligence and often haste and a woman who by necessity had her hands in every part of the business of writing, the politics of women's rights in England, the rearing of children, and the requisite creating of personas to do all of this work. Though Smith's publishers often cast her as a grubby, tiresome woman who constantly used them as her bankers in an attempt to keep her earnings to support her nine children rather than let it fall into the hands of her estranged spendthrift husband, scholars have used Smith's letters to shape different perspectives on her person. Louise Duckling reveals a Smith who is a savvy self-promoter, crafting multiple personas to serve her various needs and introduces a reading of Smith's letters and prefaces that assumes a canny wit.[10] Michael Gamer exposes Smith as a businesswoman who negotiates avenues for profit amid her authorial labors while working in a world made only for men in business and masculine concepts of authorship.[11]

In *Writing Romanticism*, Labbe explores Smith's poetic personas in greater depth, arguing for a nuanced and layered approach. When wondering if the speaker in Smith's poetry is Smith herself, Labbe introduces many other literary "selves": Smith being a poet (an artist who writes poetry), Smith as a "Poet" (a Romantic literary ideal), and Smith the Poet—the public performance persona she has created for her literary reputation.[12] That is many Smiths for us to follow. Smith's remaining papers provide ample access points for connecting her to the writing and the literary world she worked within, but they also leave us unsatisfied in their inconsistencies. Many Smith scholars could commiserate with Labbe when she evokes rapper Eminem's plea: "Will the real Charlotte Smith please stand up?"[13] But perhaps she has, as much as the fragments left over 200 years after your death can stand for you.

Smith lived to the age of 57 and enjoyed a long career. Like most people, she changed drastically over the course of her life. She was a layered, complex, and occasionally contradictory woman. She lived in tumultuous times and by necessity had to quickly change her understanding of the world around her. The Smith who published the first edition of *Elegiac Sonnets* (1784) to fund her husband's release from debtor's prison was not the same Smith who scraped together a living by writing novels after separating from him, or the Smith who revised her sonnets for decades with a poet's heart, or the Smith who explored *Beachy Head* as an experiment and a balm. Her poetry lived simultaneously, indeed likely on the same desk, with her swiftly organized novels, her angry letters to the men who oversaw the Chancery lawsuit that held up her father-in-law's bequests to her children for over 37 years, and the piles of books she used for reference.[14] We must keep this changing Smith in mind as we read her within the reviewing system, because though we may accept the right of a woman to change her mind, the Reviews did not.

Smith's popularity and tragic public persona together influenced her place in literary history as a poet, and early biographical notices of her after her death attached themselves to her later inclusion in poetical anthologies depending on how well she fit the image of tragic mother figure; she was sometimes excluded for misaligning with Victorian ideals of meek femininity.[15] Gamer and Labbe's understanding of Smith as a poet is one that is simultaneously fractured, crafted, and literary; they view her as a businesswoman, a mother, and a woman doing all of this work in a man's world. Their understanding of Smith the poet is, I think, a practical and *useful* reading that can help us understand how the reviewing system of the late eighteenth and early nineteenth centuries uniquely grappled with her and her writings. Smith's canonization as a novelist, however, came much later than her recognition as a poet and follows a different pathway that is influenced at many points by the reviewing system.

In this chapter, I first map how the material space that the Reviews devote to critiquing Smith's novels signals to us that she is an author interacting with and influenced by the reviewing system in ways that differentiate her from her novel-writing peers. Following this cue, I recontextualize the Reviews' rhetoric in their criticism of Smith considering her unique preface–review dialogue.[16] Using this recasting of the Reviews' interaction with Smith as a novelist, I trace how her preface–review dialogue contributed to the two centuries of derision directed at Smith's novels by literary critics, if they remembered to direct any attention her way at all. Reintroducing Smith's interaction with the reviewing system to her reception history, then, enables us to more clearly see Smith's legacy and helps us understand literary history's journey to knowing her.

Book reviews of Smith's work have been both peripheral to her literary output and impossible to shake. In Loraine Fletcher's thorough biography of Smith, discussion of much of her novels is "left unconsidered," along "with much contemporary comment on its author in reviews and letters, and with the history of her posthumous reputation."[17] Modern editions of Smith's sonnets reprint the high praise those works received in the Reviews, and Broadview editions of her novels include reviews in contextual materials, where they pose either as immediate reader reactions to her texts or examples of their broader critical reception. The former cannot be gleaned from a book reviewer; the latter is difficult to discern when these reviews are not read in the context of the reviewing system that produced them. And while much has been read into and from Smith's novel prefaces, they have not been considered as part of the review–preface dialogue outlined in Chapter 2, either as fitting into it or standing unique from it, when thinking about her career in relation to book reviewing.

The most attentive study thus far regarding Smith's legacy and periodicals in general is Stephen Berndt's tracing of the role they played just after Smith's death in influencing how later Romantic poets read and valued her writings, especially considering public knowledge of her personal life.[18] Additionally, Michael Gamer mindfully considers reviews as one of many forces from the literary marketplace pushing in on Smith as a new translator of novels in the late 1780s. He argues that the *Monthly*'s review of her translation *Manon Lescaut* (1786) had an effect "on Smith's subsequent literary production," causing her to title her next translation *The Romance of a Real Life* (1787) in defiance of their proclaiming *Manon* was only "really fiction."[19] This indicates Smith's keen awareness of the reviewing system's genre expectations and perhaps their influence on the literary marketplace. Curran corroborated this version of Smith, noting that "wherever readers look in her *Works*, they will find Charlotte Smith intensely engaged with the literary world she inherited, as well as the one in which she lived."[20]

Smith's prefaces and interaction with Review periodicals certainly support this understanding. Labbe's latest work endorses a reading of Smith as a *writer* rather than as a *woman writer* (emphasis mine), as most scholarship has situated her.[21] This is an important distinction that draws attention to how women writers should be located at the center of our literary, cultural, and historical studies and not relegated to separate niche readings. It is an essential movement in feminist literary studies to orient women writers to the center of our canon because of their writing, and I certainly think Smith would appreciate this move. Not every case, however, can strip away gender without losing essential context, and considering gender when orienting Smith in the reviewing system she worked in, against, and with is essential, because the business and art of novel writing was never *not* gendered and neither was the reviewing of novels.

Smith's "Rise": Sister-Queens and the Reviews

Examining how Smith and her novels were treated by the reviewing system is not a straightforward task. Smith is difficult to compare to her contemporaries, as few were so prolific or had her immediate success. Most novelists found themselves primarily noticed in the inferior Monthly Catalogue section in short reviews in the back, with the occasional successful novel featured in the Reviews' prominent front section.[22] Smith, however, achieved front billing early in her prose-writing career—her rise. After Smith published translations of two French novels, her first original novel, *Emmeline* (1788), was reviewed in the front section of both the *Critical* and the *Monthly*, as were her next several novels.

The consistency of the Reviews' attention to individual authors can be gleaned from their divided location of reviews of other popular novelists, with each periodical establishing a location trend or commitment to an author. For example, Anna Maria Bennett and Matthew "Monk" Lewis had divided but consistent review attention. Bennett was always reviewed in the front section of the *Monthly* and in the Monthly Catalogue of the *Critical*, and Lewis vice versa. Although competitors, one Review's placement of a novel's review within its pages did not seem to influence that of the other. Sheer volume of publications and general popularity also did not guarantee an author front-section review placement for their work. Eliza Parsons, for example, had 12 novels reviewed from 1790 to 1804 and never graduated beyond the Monthly Catalogue, though she was praised by both Reviews. The same was true for Elizabeth Meeke, stepsister to Frances Burney; 12 of her novels were reviewed between 1795 and 1807, all in the Monthly Catalogue. Reviews of Smith's novels during the 1790s cast her in two ways: as a once-great but forgettable novelist or as a novelist who committed unpardonable crimes against the genre. These representations of Smith shaped scholarship on her and her place in the history of the English novel until the late twentieth century. Either Smith was left out of histories entirely, overshadowed by the two writers who the Reviews identify as her peers, Burney and Ann Radcliffe, or her personal and political life were heavily focused on, her accomplishments in prose fiction an aside to their prefaces.

In the late 1780s and early 1790s, Smith was celebrated by the Reviews as a favorite, and their attention wrote her "rise" as a popular novelist into literary consciousness. After complaining for three-quarters of a page about the trouble of modern novel writers in general, the *Monthly* makes an abrupt turn in introducing Smith's first original novel to England's reading public. In the prestigious front section of their periodical, the *Monthly* notes that in reviewing *Emmeline* (1788), they had "a task very different to that in which [they] have been lately engaged." They call her "Mrs. Smith, the ingenious" and even "venture to add the *amiable* authoress" to her title.[23] The *Critical* mirrored the *Monthly*'s praise. For them, Smith was a beacon in "a new era of novel-writing." They used their front section review of *Emmeline* to "point out another example of this new species" of quality novels, one that "reflects so much credit on its author."[24]

These two front-section reviews, which also contain excerpts from the novel and are presented early in a monthly issue, argue materially for Smith's celebration as a novelist. Smith is so interesting and valuable that the Reviews privilege their attention to her in the earliest pages of their issue so that readers can prioritize them. She is not buried in the Monthly Catalogue or as the last front-section review; she is being shown off. Right away, the *Critical* compares Smith's work to that of one of the Reviews' cornerstone feminine novelists, Frances Burney: "We might, perhaps, be censured as too easy flatterers, if we said, that this novel equals Cecilia; yet we think it may stand next to Miss Burney's works, with so little inferiority." This comparison to Burney signaled to Review readers, who would have been familiar with the system's ranking of quality writers as well as the placement politics of where in an issue an article appeared, that they held Smith in high regard.

The periodicals continued to review Smith's novels in the front section and to compare her characters to Burney's. By the publication of Smith's third novel, *Celestina* (1790), the two authors' affinity is solidified when the *Critical* bestowed upon them a collective title: "In the modern school of novel-writers, Mrs. Smith holds a very distinguished rank; and, if not the first, she is so near as scarcely to be styled an inferior. Perhaps, with miss Burney she may be allowed to hold 'a divided sway;' and, though on some occasions below her *sister-queen*, yet, from the greater number of her works, she seems to possess a more luxuriant imagination, and a more fertile invention [emphasis mine]."[25] The "divided sway" quoted by the *Critical* references the prologue to Richard Brinsley Sheridan's 1779 play, *The Critic; or, A Tragedy Rehearsed*, a satire on contemporary drama and its critics. Suggesting that the pages of the Reviews were the stage of literary criticism, the *Critical* casts Burney and Smith as "sister-queens" rather than Sheridan's "Sister Muses, whom these realms obey / Who o'er Drama hold divided sway."[26] Smith, whose melancholic scenes the Reviews relish, stands in as tragedy, and Burney is their comedic ruler.

For the rest of her novel-writing career, the Reviews would regularly compare Smith to and group her with "sister-queen" novelist Burney. At times, the Reviews added a third ruler to this prose fiction kingdom: Ann Radcliffe. In 1798, the *Critical* notes: "[Smith's] stories do not agitate like the mysterious horrors of Mrs. Radcliffe; they do not divert like the lively caricatures of Mrs. D'Arblay [Burney]; but, more true to nature than either, they awaken that gentle and increasing interest which excites our feelings to the point of pleasure, not beyond it."[27] The grouping together of Smith, Burney, and Radcliffe by the Reviews in the 1790s created a well-defined standard by which novels that ranked in the upper class were to be evaluated. This triumvirate represents emerging and respectable subgenres as identified by reviewers. In their two-tier hierarchy of novel reviewing, the Reviews started out placing Smith in the upper echelon. Yet the Reviews' criticisms of Smith, who published more novels than the others of this regal cohort, changed mid-decade.

A Turn in Review Criticism

The Reviews' celebration of Smith's first novel in the front section of their periodical was unusual and marked her as a particularly skilled writer in the critics'

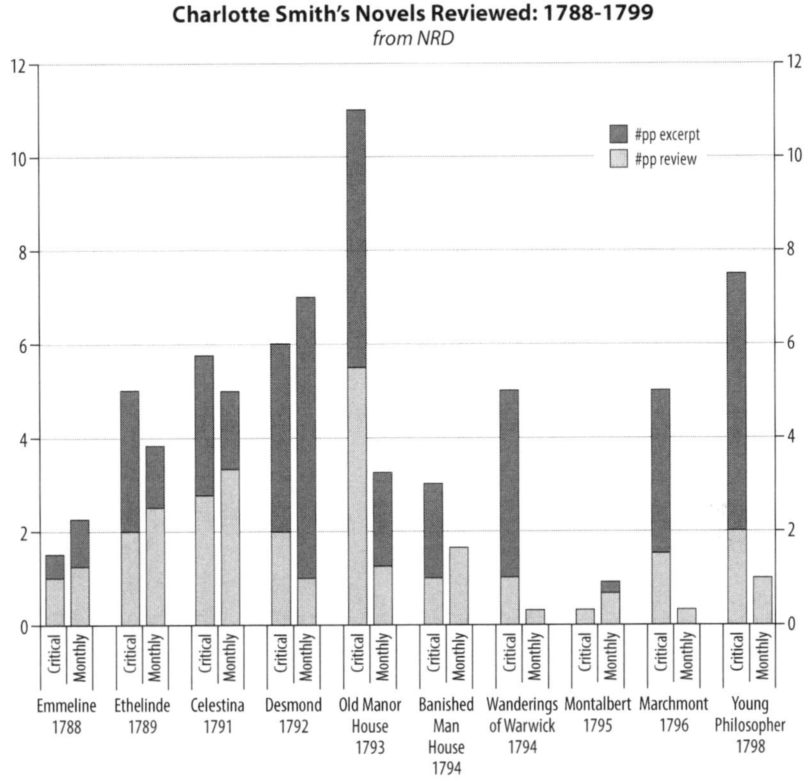

Charlotte Smith's Novels Reviewed: 1788-1799
from NRD

Figure 3.1. Charlotte Smith's Novels Reviewed from 1788–1799, pulled from the Novels Reviewed Database (NRD), 1790–1820 and relevant earlier reviews.

opinion.[28] These front-section reviews also gave over considerable page space to the original work, offering up lengthy excerpts for would-be buyers of the novel to preview. Lengthy excerpts took up significant space, and since the Reviews claimed to survey every publication of note, extended excerpts suggested that the quality of the work under review was of higher value than other works they could possibly have included in that page space, especially those in shorter Monthly Catalogue notices.[29]

The length of reviews of Smith's novels grew during her early novel-writing career. Figure 3.1 illustrates the steady climb in review length of her first four novels.[30] The *Critical* published longer reviews of novels in general than the *Monthly*, which we see reflected in their attention to Smith. In fact, Smith's early novels were receiving so much attention in length of reviews from the *Monthly* and the *Critical* that she ranked three times in the top ten longest re-

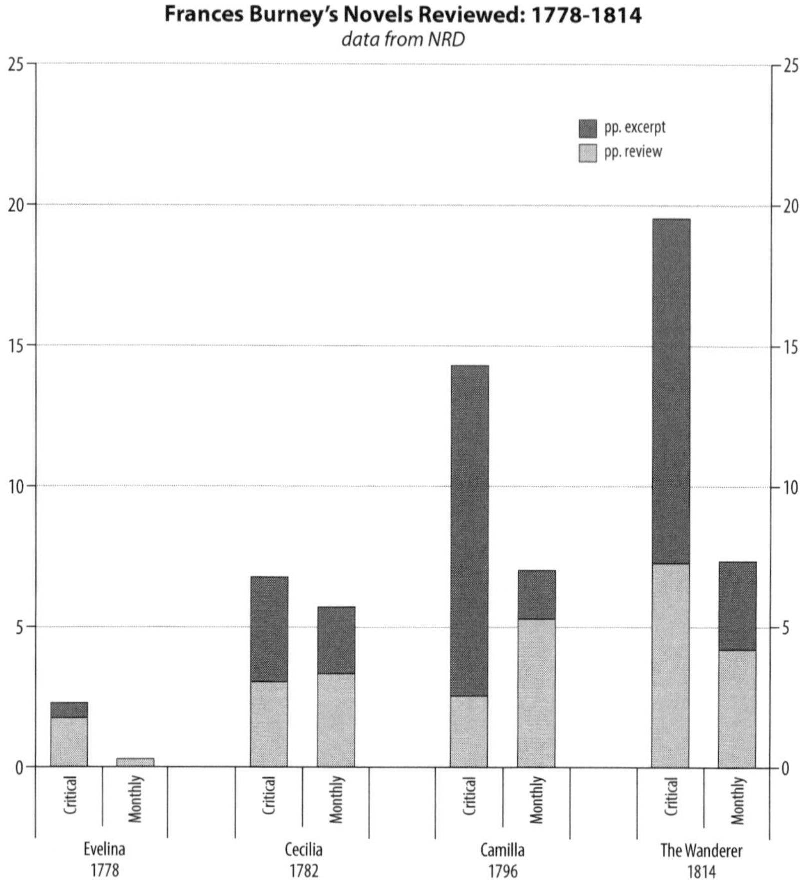

Frances Burney's Novels Reviewed: 1778-1814
data from NRD

Figure 3.2. Frances Burney's Novels Reviewed from 1778–1814, pulled from the Novels Reviewed Database (NRD), 1790–1820 and relevant earlier reviews.

views of novels from the 1790s (Table 3.2) and four times when looking only at her women contemporaries (Table 3.1). Of her novels, Smith's *Old Manor House*, her fourth original novel, receives the most attention from her oeuvre, with 11 pages from the *Critical*, the second longest review of a novel from this decade.

Unsurprisingly, the reviews of works by the other sister-queens are among the longest from this period as well. Burney's *Camilla* tops the list with 14.25 pages of attention from the *Critical* and appears again for that novel's 7-page review in the *Monthly*. Radcliffe's famously best-selling *The Mysteries of Udolpho* (1794) is third on the list, with 11 pages devoted to it in the *Critical*. This page space study aligns with the Reviews' rhetoric uplifting Burney, Smith, and Rad-

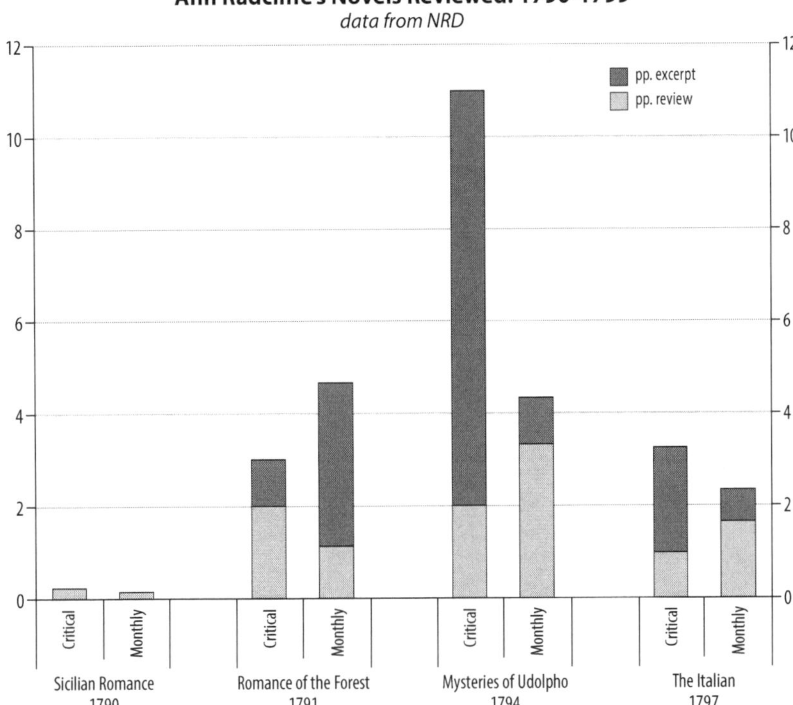

Figure 3.3. Ann Radclie's Novels Reviewed from 1790–1799, pulled from the Novels Reviewed Database (NRD), 1790–1820 and relevant earlier reviews.

cliffe as the women novelists they admired most and praised to their readers. It is notable that during the 1790s, only two male authors appear on Table 3.2 in the top ten longest novel reviews: Richard Cumberland for *Henry* (1795) and Thomas Holdcroft for *The Adventures of Hugh Trevor* (1797). In length of attention given to celebrated novelists of the 1790s, women writers reign supreme. Smith, however, is the only novelist in Table 3.1 to have more than one novel enjoy such lengthy reviews, asserting her dominance both in number of publications and in review length (where length equals quality or favor) in a crucial period of the novel's maturity as a literary genre and as a genre authored by women. Using material space to indicate the value of Smith as a novelist, the reviewing system circulated a rising authoress narrative. We can see their similar "rising" attention to Burney and Radcliffe in Figures 3.2 and 3.3.

By the Reviews' yardstick, *The Old Manor House* was the peak of Smith's novel-writing career. It would later be lauded as her best and most significant

TABLE 3.1

Novels by Women in the 1790s: Length of Reviews (excluding male novelists)
from NRD

	Author	Title	Total # Review pp.	# pp. Excerpt	# pp. Criticism	Review
1	Frances Burney	*Camilla* (1796)	14.25	11.75	2.5	*Critical*
2	Charlotte Smith	*The Old Manor House* (1793)	11	5.5	5.5	*Critical*
3	Ann Radcliffe	*The Mysteries of Udolpho* (1794)	11	9	2	*Critical*
4	Harriet & Sofia Lee	*Canterbury Tales* (1797)	7.75	6.75	1	*Critical*
5	Charlotte Smith	*The Young Philosopher* (1798)	7.5	5.5	2	*Critical*
6	Charlotte Smith	*Desmond* (1792)	7	6	1	*Monthly*
7	Frances Burney	*Camilla* (1796)	7	1.75	5.25	*Monthly*
8	Ann Yearsley	*The Royal Captives* (1795)	6.75	5	1.75	*Critical*
9	Elizabeth Inchbald	*A Simple Story* (1791)	6.33	4	2.33	*Critical*
10	Charlotte Smith	*Desmond* (1792)	6	2	4	*Critical*

TABLE 3.2

Novels in the 1790s: Length of Reviews (including male novelists)
from NRD

	Author	Novel	Total Review pp.	# pp. Excerpt	# pp. Criticism	Review
1	Frances Burney	*Camilla* (1796)	14.25	11.75	2.5	*Critical*
2	Charlotte Smith	*The Old Manor House* (1793)	11	5.5	5.5	*Critical*
3	Ann Radcliffe	*The Mysteries of Udolpho* (1794)	11	9	2	*Critical*
4	Richard Cumberland	*Henry* (1795)	8.5	6.5	2	*Critical*
5	Harriet and Sophia Lee	*Canterbury Tales* (1797)	7.75	6.75	1	*Critical*
6	Charlotte Smith	*The Young Philosopher* (1798)	7.5	5.5	2	*Critical*
7	Charlotte Smith	*Desmond* (1792)	7	6	1	*Monthly*
8	Frances Burney	*Camilla* (1796)	7	1.75	5.25	*Monthly*
9	Ann Yearsley	*The Royal Captives* (1795)	6.75	5	1.75	*Critical*
10	Thomas Holcroft	*The Adventures of Hugh Trevor* (1797)	6.75	2.25	4.5	*Monthly*

TABLE 3.3
Longest Novel Reviews by Decade, 1790–1820
from NRD

	1790s	1800s	1810s
1	Frances Burney *Camilla* (1796)	Translator Unknown (original author: August Friedrich Ferdinand von Kotzebue) *The Pastor's Daughter* (1807)	Sir Walter Scott *The Monastery* (1820)
2	Charlotte Smith *The Old Manor House* (1793)	Hannah More *Coelebs In Search of A Wife* (1808)	Frances Burney *The Wanderer* (1814)
3	Ann Radcliffe *The Mysteries of Udolpho* (1794)	Matthew Gregory Lewis *Romantic Tales* (1808)	Charles Brockden Brown *Wieland* (1814)
4	Richard Cumberland *Henry* (1795)	Anonymous *Delphine* (1803)	Sir Walter Scott *Ivanhoe* (1820)
5	Harriet and Sophia Lee *The Canterbury Tales* (1797)	Thomas Holcroft *Memoirs of Bryan Perdue* (1805)	Sir Walter Scott *The Abbot* (1820)
6	Charlotte Smith *The Young Philosopher* (1798)	Elizabeth Hamilton *The Cottagers of Glenburnie* (1808)	Sir Walter Scott *Rob Roy* (1818)
7	Charlotte Smith *Desmond* (1792)	Hannah More *Coelebs In Search of A Wife* (1808)	Sir Walter Scott *The Antiquary* (1816)
8	Frances Burney *Camilla* (1796)	Sophie Ristaud Cottin *Claire d'Albe* (1808)	Sir Walter Scott *Waverley* (1814)
9	Ann Yearsley *The Royal Captives* (1797)	Robert Charles Dallas *The Morlands* (1805)	Jane Porter *The Pastor's Fire Side* (1817)
10	Thomas Holcroft *The Adventures of Hugh Trevor* (1795)	Sophia Lee *The Life of a Lover* (1804)	Charles Robert Maturin *Women* (1818)

novel and is the one included in most selected novel collections or quoted in nineteenth- and twentieth-century excerpts of her prose works. Smith's repeated success in the 1790s should have marked her for the same level of canonicity and notoriety as her sister-queens. A broader study of the length of novel reviews by decade (Table 3.3) shows for the 1800s a group of writers and works who would appear repeatedly in early anthologies of the novel—Hannah More appearing twice for *Coelebs In Search of A Wife* (1808) and two popular novelists listed for their less-memorable novels, Lewis's *Romantic Tales* (1808; the author is better known for *The Monk*, 1796) and Sophia Lee's *The Life of a Lover* (1804;

better known for *The Recess*, 1783).[31] Five of the top ten longest reviews for the 1800s are of novels by women and two are of works by anonymous authors/ translators. Table 3.3 shows that by 1820, the works that receive the most review attention are by men, who hold eight of the top ten longest review spots (six of those are held by Scott).[32] Scott would go on to be perhaps the most famous novelist from the Romantic period as well as the editor of one of the first English novels collections that worked to build a lasting narrative about the genre during that time.

A quantitative look at Smith as an equal data point to this cohort of novelists by their length of review attention, however, does not convey the changing and nuanced role the Reviews had in writing her reputation in print for the contemporary reading public and literary history. On the surface, Table 3.1 shows multiple points of success for Smith across a decade, but a close study of the gap of five years between the success of *Old Manor House* (1793) and the appearance on this table of *The Young Philosopher* (1798) holds some explanation for Smith's absence from early novel canonicity and the "fall" of her story as a novelist, as implied by Fry. In the mid-1790s, Smith faced a changing political landscape that caused her to alter her own outspoken perspectives. She was under continued financial strain, which, combined with her politics, also put her in the position of shifting publishers—something Smith saw as personal and professional misfortune. Further, Smith was herself unwell at this time and facing great loss in her family life, nursing one child and burying another. This storm of change and sorrow colored her literary output, placing it at odds with the Reviews' cultural expectations, and clarifies the five-year gap shown in Table 3.2 and the dip in Review attention in Figure 3.1.

In its early years, Smith was sympathetic to the French Revolution. She supported the rights of the oppressed lower classes across the channel.[33] Her novel in reaction to the early Revolutionary years, *Desmond* (1792), was deeply controversial in England.[34] This epistolary novel is set in France between 1790 and 1792 and follows an abused married woman, estranged from her husband, whom the young titular character pursues amid the chaos of those years. The Reviews' strong reaction to such a blatantly political and morally questionable novel from the pen of the sister-queen they had praised for her sentimental tales is evident in their voluminous attention to this text. But like many English sympathizers, Smith was appalled by the bloody methods used to enact change in France, which she felt contradictory to revolutionary sentiment. The execution of Louis XVI in January 1793, just six months after the publication of *Desmond*, and the ensuing Reign of Terror caused Smith to reconsider her political associations.

In her following novels, especially *The Banished Man* (1794) and *Marchmont* (1796), Smith turned her revolutionary eye to England. Instead of the fervent voice for a regime change she volleyed at France in *Desmond*, her later political works included an examination of the need for social change in her home country centered on property, inheritance, and the wrongs of women—all of which further highlighted her own financial and marital struggles.

For these mid-decade novels, Smith was also required to hastily shift for publishers willing to put out her heated political texts. After publishing almost exclusively with Thomas Cadell Sr. to this point, she had to turn to other publishers for *Desmond* (George Robinson), *Old Manor House* (Joseph Bell), *Wanderings of Warwick* (Joseph Bell), *Montalbert* (Sampson Low), and *Marchmont* (Sampson Low). None had the reputation of Cadell, and all were wholly unsympathetic to Smith's ongoing personal and financial struggles; Bell even had her arrested for breach of contract. Smith's favorite publisher, Cadell Sr., was unwilling to publish *Desmond*, due to both its politics and Smith's continued need to use her publishers as her bankers. He was worn out by serving as Smith's go-between and advocate. But Smith worked hard to maintain her connection to the Cadell firm, which went on to publish her poem *The Emigrants* in 1793 and her novel *The Banished Man* in 1794. This may be because Cadell Sr. sympathized with the marital and financial strife Smith was experiencing at the time.

Though always living under the financial strain that her paltry income and unresolved inheritance settlement left her, Smith endured some particularly difficult years in the mid-1790s. Her furious writing and publishing pace attests to her continued need for funds, and the short length of these novels highlights what a difficult time she was having writing, considering the hardships she faced. In July 1793, her son Charles returned to her with a permanent disability, having lost a leg in the siege of Dunkirk. Smith wrote to Cadell Sr. in December of that year, expressing her hope to secure medical attention in Bath for Charles: "If I could sell the Book I am writing for a certain Sum . . . I might possibly continue to pay for a lodging [in Bath] for a month or six weeks."[35] She pitched *The Banished Man* to Cadell Sr., hoping he would purchase the copyright so she would not have to return to Bell. Cadell Sr. did step up, but Smith's fortunes did not improve. Her favorite daughter, Anna Augusta, became increasingly ill with tuberculosis, and much of Smith's time and emotional energy was spent nursing her. Anna Augusta had married a French emigrant in 1793, probably further influencing the Smith family's sympathy for the victims of the Reign of Terror and the First Republic. While nursing Charles and Anna

TABLE 3.4
Location of Reviews of Smith's Novels
from NRD

Novel	*Monthly* Location	*Critical* Location
Ethelinde (1789)	F	F
Celestina (1791)	F	F
Desmond (1792)	F	F
Old Manor House (1793)	F	F
Banished Man (1794)	F	F
Wanderings of Warwick (1794)	MC	F
Montalbert (1795)	MC	MC
Marchmont (1796)	MC	F
The Young Philosopher (1798)	MC	F
Letters of a Solitary Wanderer (1800) vols I–III	MC	F
Letters of a Solitary Wanderer (1802) vols IV–V	MC	F

MC=Monthly Catalogue; F=Front Section of Review

Augusta, Smith published novels with Bell and Low that were shorter than her earlier four- to five-volume sentimental novels. *Desmond* and *Montalbert* were both three volumes; *The Wanderings of Warwick* was an almost unheard-of one volume. Anna Augusta died in childbirth at age 20 in April 1795, just as Smith was completing *Montalbert*.[36] Smith was devastated.

The political content and shorter length of the novels Smith wrote during this period partly explain the dip in attention the reviewing system gave to her works, reflected in Figure 3.1. Each of the Reviews would handle Smith's period of change differently, but their reactions would influence how Smith was remembered by later critics of the novel. The *Monthly Review*'s reaction was to relocate their reviews of Smith's novels to the Monthly Catalogue, beginning with the one-volume *Wanderings of Warwick* (Table 3.4). For the *Monthly*, this signaled an about-face in their attention to Smith. Their Jacobin leanings could be part of this shift—possibly they were disappointed in Smith's changing revolutionary sentiments. For example, they note with discontent of her earlier *The Old Manor House* that "once or twice, but very sparingly, political ideas and opinions are introduced, and the author takes occasion to express that generous spirit of freedom which is displayed more at large in her *Desmond*."[37] They praise her politics in *Desmond*, stating she is "very justly of opinion, that the great events which are passing in the world are no less interesting to women than to men."[38] The *Monthly*'s change in location of Smith's reviews may also signal their frustration with *The Wandering of Warwick*'s short length. The relocation of their reviews to the Monthly Catalogue, however, unarguably illustrates that

Smith was no longer considered among that upper tier of novelists whose writing deserved space in the front section of their Review.[39]

Reviewing Smith's novels in the Monthly Catalogue was, for the *Monthly*, a permanent demotion. Their recognition of *The Wanderings of Warwick* is not unfavorable but also does not include the protracted praise they previously gave Smith. They call the work "a mere supplement to the former novel of the Old Manor House," and the critic quickly moves on to the next novel under review in that back section.[40] Smith never regained her ground with the *Monthly*. Their very last words on her as a novelist, a scant five lines from the review of her 1802 continued volumes of *Letters of a Solitary Wanderer* (volumes I and II were published in 1800), are to inform readers "they need scarcely be told, they will derive an addition to that entertainment which the writings of Mrs. Smith always afford."[41] The reviewer evidently felt that previous positive mentions of Smith's novels were enough to last her a lifetime.

The *Monthly*'s relocation of their reviews of her fiction to the Monthly Catalogue is reflected in the sharp drop in number of review pages shown in Figure 3.1. This change is also reflected in the content of the articles: reviews in the Monthly Catalogue seldom included excerpts. The *Monthly*'s act of moving recognitions of Smith's novels was unique considering they had previously showered her with such praise. Neither of Smith's sister-queen novelists received such varying attention from the Reviews across their careers (Table 3.5), but neither included such blatant political sentiments in their texts nor published such short novels.

Unlike the *Monthly*, the *Critical* maintained its devotion to reviewing Smith's novels in the front section of their periodical. They responded to her many mid-decade life and career changes with a new mix of criticism undiscernible from

TABLE 3.5
Location of Novel Reviews
from NRD

	Frances Burney			Ann Radcliffe		
Novel	*Critical* location	*Monthly* location	Novel	*Critical* location	*Monthly* location
---	---	---	---	---	---
Evelina (1778)	F	MC	*A Sicilian Romance* (1790)	MC	MC
Cecilia (1782)	F	F	*Romance of the Forest* (1791)	F	F
Camilla (1796)	F	F	*Mysteries of Udolpho* (1794)	F	F
The Wanderer (1814)	F	F	*The Italian* (1797)	F	F

MC=Monthly Catalogue; F=Front Section of Review

a quantitative study of review location, length, or even a straightforward look at how much criticism she received. As Table 3.4 shows, the *Critical* committed themselves to their past promotions of Smith's novels in the front section of their journal, demonstrating a loyalty to the author. They insist that even when they do not find *Old Manor House* of the top variety, "as it is a production of a lady who has already furnished the public with several ingenious performances, and who has obtained a very considerable share of public approbation; we conceived ourselves called upon to deliver our sentiments at some length on a subject to which we seldom dedicate so large a portion of our Review."[42] While they devote page space and prime review location to the novel, they are reluctant to continue their previous rhetorical praise of Smith. The *Critical* only once consigns Smith to the Monthly Catalogue for her *Montalbert* in August 1797, and on this occasion, they claim that "by some accident this novel has hitherto escaped our notice,—a circumstance we ought to regret, as it might have sooner relieved us from the inundation of romantic horrors with which the press has lately groaned."[43]

This Review's continued attention to Smith across the 1790s is puzzling in one way: The *Critical* had historically Tory and High Church leanings. Their continued delegation of page space to Smith, who was herself Whiggish and whose writing was filled with revolutionary sympathies, seems contradictory. It is also surprising that their attention to Smith's most political novel, *Desmond*, is comparable in page length to the *Monthly*'s (six pages to the *Monthly*'s seven). While the *Monthly*'s review of *Desmond* features six pages of excerpts from the novel, however, the *Critical*'s review features more pages of criticism. In these pages, the *Critical*'s disapproving tone would influence the narrative of Smith's "fall" as a novelist and set the stage for her personal life and political sentiments to overshadow her literary efforts. The material the *Critical* found to fuel their discussion came from Smith herself. During these tumultuous mid-decade years that pressed on her personally and professionally, Smith took to her pen to share these frustrations with readers in the space provided for literary authors to engage with critics and the reading public: her prefaces.

Prefaces and Personal Life in the Reviews

Like those of her contemporaries, Smith's novel prefaces are spaces where she engages with the titans of literary criticism, preemptively considering those areas they most criticized in the works of women writers. As the previous chapter notes, these prefaces often serve as catalysts for a dialogue with the Reviews, where the authoresses could drive a back-and-forth exchange in print about

subjects of their choosing. After enjoying a quiet (on Smith's end) and congenial relationship with the reviewing system across their articles praising her first
three novels, Smith anticipates the blowback her political *Desmond* will receive
and bursts loudly into the ongoing preface–review dialogue tradition.[44] Smith
was already using the prefaces of her *Elegiac Sonnets* to make generally known
the financial hardships that she and her children faced, and those print spaces
became what Sarah Zimmerman calls "a serialized autobiographical narrative."[45] The fact that she took up her pen in the preceding pages of *Desmond*,
then, can be no surprise to us, as she was a seasoned writer who was well aware
of the reviewing system she was working within.

In an extreme act of defense against the possibility of being accused of trea-
son for the political sentiments in the novel, Smith states in the preface to
Desmond: "As to the political passages dispersed though the work, they are for
the most part, drawn from conversations to which I have been witness in England, and France." But with her politics, she insists, "the Public have nothing
to do: but were it proper to relate all the disadvantages from anxiety of mind
and local circumstances, under which these volumes have been composed, such
a detail might be admitted as an excuse for more material errors."[46] Novelists
of the 1790s who used fiction as an innocuous cover from prosecution against
writing political work relied on its popularity to spread ideas to readers. These
political motivations also parallel those of popular novelists like Smith, who
relied on being widely read enough to earn money but wanted to meet high
literature standards to avoid being derided by the reviews.[47] *Desmond*'s preface
illustrates Smith having to walk this line.

The Reviews respond, engaging in a conversation with Smith on what con-
stituted appropriate novel subjects and the level to which she shared her private
trials. The *Critical* and the *Monthly* both directly refer to *Desmond*'s preface in
their pages and use it as an opportunity to scold Smith. The *Monthly*'s dialogue
with Smith's prefaces begins reservedly. They express their disappointment in
her political writing. "As we have formerly had repeated occasions to express
our favourable opinion of Mrs. Smith's general talents for novel-writing," they
note, they let her off with only a small reprimand for the content of *Desmond*.
Their collective voice insists that "we confine ourselves, in our extracts" to those
passages that come, as "Mrs. S. assures the public in her preface, from conversations to which she has been witness in England and in France, during the last
twelve months"—quoting her preface directly.[48] The *Critical* is more direct:
"Indeed, in all her novels, the descriptions of scenery and situation are pecu-
liarly excellent," but "her politics we cannot always approve of." They insist that

"connect[ion] with the reformers, and the revolutionists" has brought her down in their esteem. "She has borrowed her colouring from them," they state, disappointed.[49] Following *Desmond*, dialogue between Smith's prefaces and the Reviews turned hostile.

While the Reviews express their displeasure with the political content of Smith's subsequent novels, their dialogue is deeply enmeshed with arguments about what is socially acceptable and expected of professional women writers and the literature they produced. Smith participates in the preface trends reflected in the previous chapter's Table 2.1. By requesting the leniency of critics, Smith shows her awareness that "reviewers over-exaggerate the moral identification between women writers and the novels they produce," as Hannah Doherty Hudson asserts, and that their criticisms "emphasise the connections between women's fiction and other aspects of women's lives."[50] A reading of Smith's reviews–prefaces dialogue necessarily considers the degree to which she shared her private (familial, legal, financial) troubles in her prefaces (and even used her life as fodder for her plots and characters) and how the Reviews responded to this entangling of the personal and the professional.

In the preface to *The Banished Man* (1794), Smith picks up the conversation left off with *Desmond*'s reviews: "In the strictures on a late publication of mine, some Review (I do not now recollect which) objected to the too frequent allusion I made in it to my own circumstances."[51] Her preface not only reminds the Reviews of their chiding but also points any reader of this novel to those criticisms. She invites readers to view the public brawl between her prefaces and review criticism. And, despite Smith's prefatory explanations, the Reviews refuse to let the matter drop. They are dead set against Smith's monopolizing her novel's plot and prefaces with her autobiography, and they mean to tell her so. Shaming her for writing for both profit and to further her own political ideals, the *Critical* accuses her of a third sin they deem to be far worse—"to give vent to her feelings, and claim the sympathy of the public for the distresses and perplexities of her private concerns."[52] This is in reference to Smith's statement in the novel's preface that she needs to "provide for the necessities of a large family, almost entirely by my own labour" due to the "injustice and evasion on the part of those who have detained the property of my children from them."[53] The *Monthly*'s response is again more reserved. "Considerable indulgence is due" to her situation, they say. Though her "domestic troubles," as they call them, "may not enhance the intrinsic value of her productions," readers should remember "that what the heart feels strongly, the tongue and the pen will not easily refrain from expressing."[54] In this clash, we see the Reviews and Smith's prefaces discussing her personal life in conjunction with what makes a good novel and even what was appropriate material for the preface.

But Smith's prefaces kept her personal life before the eyes of readers and critics and were a space where she manipulated chivalric ideals of rescuing spurned women into a marketing device, albeit one the Reviews grew tired of.[55] In the preface of her ninth novel, *Marchmont* (1796), Smith reminds us that this is her "thirty-second volume now before the Public," and her experience with speaking across the borders of her prefaces and the Reviews is evident.[56] "Few things perhaps are more difficult than to write a preface well," Smith tells us in the opening line. "And it is perhaps equally true," she goes on to say, "that no part of the book is so little read." Yet since Smith's prefaces were clearly the catalyst for the snapping conversation she participated in across textual borders with the literary critics, she cannot have thought these pages so neglected. "I wish for an occasion to address my readers, or such of them as will take the trouble of perusing a few prefatory pages," Smith slyly comments, verily aware that all readers of her work by then knew to look to her prefaces for animated details of her life. And of course, the Reviews would "take the trouble of perusing a few prefatory pages," as they were her primary audience.

She calls back to the *Critical*'s infuriation with her interpolating her life's sorrows into her text when stating defensively that this practice, "though less excusable in the body of work, may be allowed [in the preface], because no one is compelled to read it to the interruption of the story, and none can complain that, as in another work, with fictitious sorrows I have mingled my own."[57] And while the *Critical* reviews *Marchmont* in the front review section and offers some excerpts, they have fallen out of love with Smith. The *Monthly* gives this novel only a quarter-page nod in the Monthly Catalogue, saying standoffishly that "nothing written by Mrs. Smith, for the rational entertainment of the public, has ever yet, within our recollection, failed of producing the effect intended."[58] This passive-aggressive review cites their disappointment with Smith's latest novels and prefaces. With their dig at her subject and style, the *Monthly* argues that she is no longer writing "for the rational entertainment of the public" but has become irrational. This gendered criticism of a female writer, struggling across her prefaces to defend her livelihood, signals Smith's fall from grace. The Reviews use their authority to declare Smith unsound, effectively insisting that any who wrote against their enforced genre boundaries, either in style or in overt dialogue through authorial prefaces, must be unhinged.

While Table 3.4 shows the decrease in attention that the *Monthly* gave Smith when they moved her reviews to the Monthly Catalogue, it fails to adequately reflect Smith's unique case of personal interaction with Reviews and how it should be read in the reviewing system. Similarly, the page space tracked in Figure 3.1 does not tell the whole story. While Figure 3.1 underlines the *Critical*'s commitment to providing excerpts of Smith's novels, it also highlights the page-space dominance (both in review and excerpt) of *Old Manor House*. Notably, reviews of Smith's novels often include excerpts of greater or equal length to the pages of criticism. This underscores Smith's general popularity—Review subscribers did not need to be enticed to read reviews of Smith's novels; indeed, the Reviews seemed to be a place to preview Smith's latest work, as so many pages of excerpt were devoted to her publications. The *Monthly* became disenchanted with her after the publication of *The Wanderings of Warwick*, and the *Critical* remained committed to Smith, unwilling to abandon an author they had once so vehemently supported. If the *Critical* was sympathetic to Smith's troubles, they do not say so in their review of *Warwick*, but the content of this review is rigidly traditional. That is, it contains *only* criticism of the novel under review and excerpts of that novel. This stands out only when we consider the effect of Smith's preface–review dialogue on the content of their reviews of her novels.

While criticism of the work and excerpts from it were the established and lauded formulas for novel reviews, where Smith was concerned, this was not always the case.[59] Figure 3.1 (and Figs. 3.2 and 3.3 for Burney and Radcliffe) tracks only the page space of the two traditional review elements: criticism and excerpt. A cursory review of the data tracking the material element of page space might suggest that because the *Monthly* decreased the pages it devoted to Smith's novels, it had the greater influence on narrating her "fall." However, the content of these reviews—especially those of the *Critical*, who kept reviewing Smith's novels at length—and the arguments these translated to Romantic readers through the literary system of book reviewing cannot be ignored. Figure 3.4 tracks the subject matter of the reviews' page space when critiquing Smith's novels. By the Reviews' own formula, each review should consist only of criticism of the novel and an excerpt from that work. But as Figure 3.4 establishes, three additional subject categories are present in reviews of Smith's novels: criticism of genre, criticism of Smith's politics, and commentary on Smith's personal life. Still on topic for the periodicals' mission is criticism of the genre. The two other sections that appear in reviews of Smith's novels are not related to the mission of the Reviews and seldom appear in reviews of other authors: criticism of the author's politics and commentary on her life. Comparable figures for Radcliffe and Burney are not provided because the categories appear-

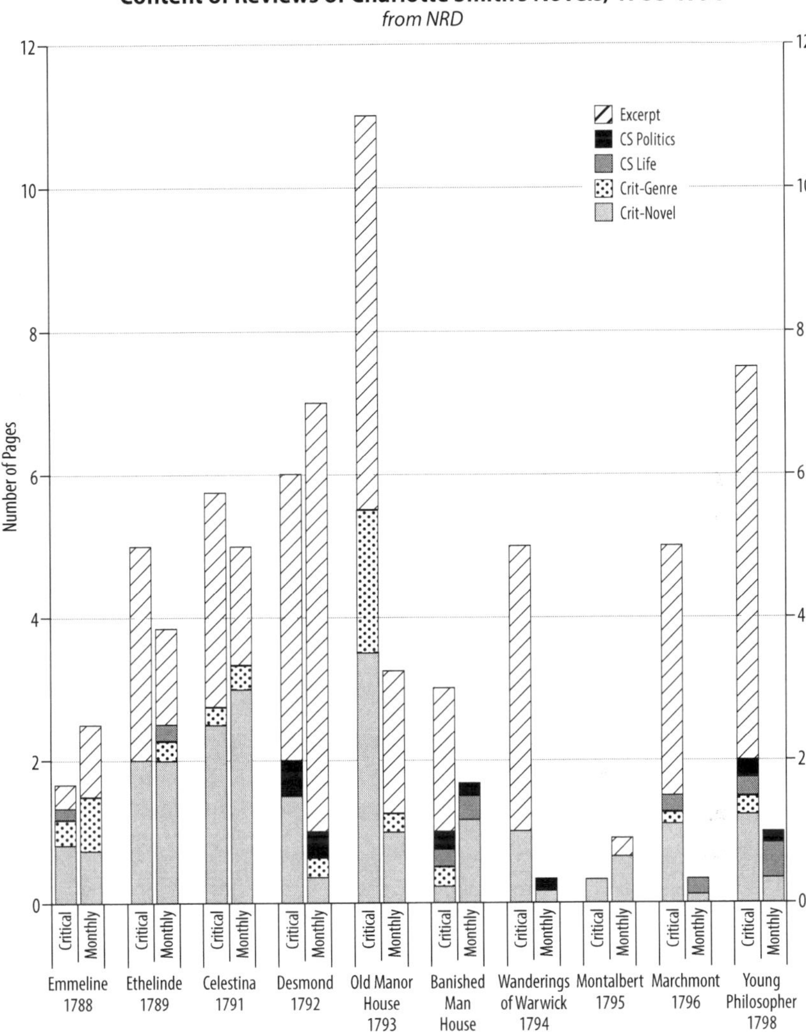

Figure 3.4. Charlotte Smith's Novels Reviewed from 1788–1798, pulled from the Novels Reviewed Database (NRD), 1790–1820 and relevant earlier reviews.

ing here in Smith's reviews account for a mere half-sentence in a single review for each. Criticism of Smith's personal life and politics, however, in a Review that claimed to focus on literary merits and served England's reading public as a repository of literature set the tone for *all* future criticisms of Smith's novels and legitimized her personal and political life as viable topics of scrutiny.

Early reviews of Smith's novels include short references to her domestic upheaval. The *Critical*'s review of *Emmeline* states only, "We hope that she has not looked at home, in the misfortunes of Mrs. Stafford."[60] Over time, as Smith revealed more about her private life in her prefaces, the reviews' comments grew longer as well. Notably, Figure 3.4 affirms that the emergence of these additional review subject categories often align with the novels that Smith prefixed with a preface: *Ethelinde* (1789, includes a dedication), *Desmond* (1792), *The Banished Man* (1794), *Marchmont* (1796), *The Young Philosopher* (1798), and *Letters of a Solitary Wanderer* (1800). Just as select collections would include (in the mode of Samuel Johnson's *Lives of the Most Eminent English Poets*) a biographical preface, the Reviews' habit of discussing Smith's novels and Smith herself set the tone for her rise-and-fall narrative. Smith's entering into dialogue with the Reviews through her novels' paratext established the lasting tradition of biographizing Smith for her life's trials and political interests when discussing the unfortunate "fall" of her novel-writing career. Smith, then, influenced the reviews and their content. Her own willingness to participate in a sharp dialogue with the Reviews across her prefaces eventually influenced modern scholarship about her. It is worth noting, however, that Smith's extant writings show what her sister-queens' could not—that a woman without the guarantees of a stable marriage and financial security or male patronage in the publishing world (such as Burney had in her father) had no choice but to reveal the absolute complexities of her life and persona, to lean on them whenever and however she could to make her living.

Smith was certainly not alone in supporting herself with her novel writing or by using her own life experiences to inform her stories. Smith was also not the only writer who received backlash from the Reviews, which were, as Hudson notes, "projecting their beliefs about these women's lives, skills, and characters on to their professional assessments of female writing."[61] Smith's case, because of her contemporary popularity, magnifies the situation and illustrates the degree to which the reviewing system amplified gendered expectations of novelists and their works and thereby influenced subsequent centuries of criticism of those women writers.

Remembering Smith's "Fall"

The Reviews' treatment of Smith as a novelist was replicated in early canon-building efforts to create a cohesive collection of the English novel across the next two centuries. These collections in turn served as the source texts for scholarship about the genre in the early twentieth century, thereby stretching the reviewing system's influence over Smith's literary legacy into our current work. As Clifford Siskin notes of the Reviews, their hand in the "Great Forgetting" of women writers was due in no small part to their emphasis on masculine expectations of authorship.[62] Other periodicals, like *The Lady's Magazine*, had a hand in writing women's literary history by reprinting texts, keeping them "current," and circulating biographies. However, Jennie Batchelor shows that the disparity between our modern canon and the once popular women writers filling the pages of eighteenth-century periodicals means that feminist recovery work has yet to excavate the extent of these source materials' role in this history.[63] And certainly Romantic contemporaries were already turning to periodicals to build the canon of English prose fiction, even as it was still being written.

Materially, the front section of the Reviews contributed to the "eighteenth-century's 'need' for an ordered canon." Gamer notes how this canon "found . . . potent expression through an already existing and heavily commodified publisher's vehicle: the multi-volume, many-authored form . . . the 'select collection.'"[64] The front section Reviews operated in the same function as select collections of novels by creating a literary hierarchy. While the Monthly Catalogue merely noted that a text existed, a front-section review provided an excerpt— thereby making the text (or part of it, at least) *literally* exist in another place.[65] This surrogate reprint is like an abridged edition and is certainly part of a work's textual history, providing plot summary and criticism of its place in the history of the genre. Recognition in the front section of the Reviews was often, therefore, a novel's first inclusion in a select collection.

Early nineteenth-century select collections of the novel mirror the Reviews' handling of Smith in their treatment and inclusion (or exclusion) of her works. Barbauld's 50-volume *The British Novelists* (1810) (Appendix A) was the first collection to set out as a complete (not reliant on serialization) canon of the British novel. In *British Novelists*, Barbauld organized two narratives simultaneously: a hierarchy and a history of the genre.[66] Barbauld notably includes very recent publications, up to Maria Edgeworth's 1805 *The Modern Griselda*, arguing that important contributions to the novel were still coming and were authored by women. The included works and Barbauld's "biographical notices and critical remarks" proceed in almost chronological form, but her disruptions signal significant contributions.[67] For example, Barbauld starts the series with Samuel Richardson rather than Daniel Defoe, weighting Richardson's longer epistolary works as the novel's genesis rather than *Robinson Crusoe*. Barbauld places Clara Reeve's contribution to the Gothic before its predecessor by Horace

Walpole, a move that highlights that subgenre's alignment with feminine authorship. Smith's *Old Manor House* (1793; vols. 36–37) is also a disruptor of chronology, appearing after John Moore's *Zeluco* (1789) but before Burney's novels *Evelina* (1778) and *Cecilia* (1782).[68]

Barbauld places Smith first out of the sister-queens, casting her as the origin of these three, though her legacy would be so different. The *British Novelists* replicated the Reviews' grouping of these three powerhouse women novelists of the late eighteenth century and adopted the Reviews' rhetoric where Smith was concerned. *Old Manor House* is the only novel of Smith's included in Barbauld's collection, whereas Burney and Radcliffe each have two (*Evelina, Cecilia*; *Romance of the Forest, Mysteries of Udolpho*). Considering Figure 3.1 and Figure 3.4's assessment of the Reviews' page space devoted to *Old Manor House*, it is no surprise that this was the novel Barbauld chose. The *Critical* devotes two pages to positioning *Old Manor House* in their discussion of the genre—a position that Barbauld would ratify and reproduce in her collection.

In her prefaces, Barbauld tells a story about each novel and its author's importance and contribution to the history of the genre in Britain. Though it is possible that copyright issues of Smith's later novels may have caused their exclusion, there is in fact evidence to the contrary. Works from the publishers of Smith's other novels appear in Barbauld's collection by other writers: Cadell (Smith's *Emmeline, Ethelinde, Celestina, The Banished Man*, and *The Young Philosopher*) published both of the included Henry Mackenzie novels (*The Man of Feeling* in 1771 and *Julia de Roubigne* in 1777), John Moore's *Zeluco* (1789), and Burney's *Cecilia* (1782); Robinson (Smith's *Desmond*) published both novels by Elizabeth Inchbald (*A Simple Story* in 1791 and *Nature and Art* in 1796) and Radcliffe's *Mysteries of Udolpho*. Therefore, copyright issues cannot have been what induced Barbauld to forego these works.[69]

Barbauld argues that Smith's "most finished novels" were *Emmeline* and *Celestina*, yet she chose *Old Manor House* for her collection because it "is said to be the most popular of the author's productions."[70] She devotes a single paragraph to situating *Old Manor House* in Smith's literary output, stating generally of Smith's novels that they "all show a knowledge of life, and facility of execution" and lamenting only that they are often "without very strong features, or particularly aiming to illustrate any moral truth."[71] This assessment of *Old Manor House* and Smith's novels in general draws on the *Monthly*'s rhetoric of 1793: "In fine, though we cannot say that we think the present novel *superior* to those which Mrs. S. has formerly produced, yet it discovers, in a considerable degree, facility of invention, knowledge of life, and command of language."[72]

The *Critical* also comes to these conclusions with their praise for Smith's general talent as a novelist: "The dignified sentiments of the human breast are touched with no unskilful [*sic*] hand." The Review then laments that *Old Manor House* had less of a moral underpinning than her previous works: "While youthful thoughtlessness and intemperance are crowned with success, ingratitude and the most complicated villainy remain unpunished."[73]

Barbauld's inclusion of Smith's peak-reviewed *Old Manor House* and a discussion focused only on her earlier novels reinforces the rise and fall outlined by the Reviews. By 1810, the Reviews' late 1790s responses to Smith's novels had already influenced her earliest opportunity to be named in the canon of the English novel. Barbauld recognizes Smith's later novels only in a list—"*Desmond, The Wanderings of Warwick, Montalbert,* and many others"—leaving out entirely *The Banished Man, Marchmont,* and *The Young Philosopher.* In remembering Smith, Barbauld has also reproduced the Reviews' disappointment in the inclusion of her politics and personal trials when she states that Smith's "later works would have been more pleasing, if the author, in the exertions of fancy, could have forgotten herself; but the asperity of invective and querulousness of complaint too frequently cloud the happier exertions of her imagination."[74]

Following Barbauld's *British Novelists* came Ballantyne's *Novelist's Library* (1821–1824) (Appendix A) with biographical notes by Scott. If the Reviews established Smith's rise-and-fall narrative, which Barbauld perpetuated, it was Scott who cemented it. The influence of the Ballantyne's series is that it includes "Scott's novelists." Scott's authorship of the *Waverley* series was an open secret, and his name did for Ballantyne's what Johnson's did for the *British Poets.* It is suggested that this was Scott's personal library of great novelists, and as a novelist himself, he endowed this collection a certain authority.[75] Smith was not included in Scott's *Novelist's Library*; neither is Burney. But Scott did not cut out women entirely: Reeve and Radcliffe both earn space in the ten-volume collection.[76] Scott did draft a biographical introduction for Smith, but scholars remain undecided as to whether he intended to include this in the *Novelist's Library* before room ran out, who "rejected" Smith from the collection (Scott or the publishers), or if it was always meant for its eventual home, *Miscellaneous Prose Works* (1826).[77] Like Barbauld's biography and all biographical remembrances of Smith thereafter, Scott's piece on Smith draws heavily on the 1801 notice of her in *Public Characters of 1801,* talking extensively about Smith's tumultuous marriage.[78] Further, Scott himself did not actually write the final version of Smith's biographical sketch. He outsourced a revision to Smith's sister, Catherine Anne Dorset.

Being left out of Scott's *Novelist's Library*, a collection that gave authority to a declarative English canon of novelists, ultimately placed Smith beneath women writers like Radcliffe, whom Scott did include, in the hierarchy of late eighteenth-century contributors to that genre's formation. Scott authorized the Reviews' representation of Smith's fall, which overshadowed her early success, and sanctioned a canon that excluded her works, despite her extensive number of contributions, popularity, and reigning place next to Burney and Radcliffe in the 1790s. Scott's influence was so far-reaching that early twentieth-century critics were still claiming that "by far the best criticism of the eighteenth century novelists will be found in the prefatory notices contributed by Scott to *Balantyne's Novelist's Library*."[79] Discussions of Smith across the nineteenth century repeat a narrative of her fall and give significant attention to her personal life and political beliefs in spaces that claim to focus on literary work.[80] From Sir E. Brydges's *Censura Literraria* (1815) to Jane Williams's *The Literary Women of England* (1861), attention to Smith's writing replicates Review arguments, conveying disappointment in the failure of her later novels and engaging in extended discussion of her life beyond her literature.

The grieving for Smith's lost place in the history of the novel and her "fall" as a novelist began a mere ten years after Scott's *Novelist's Library* appeared. In an 1836 gift book, *The Token and Atlantic Souvenir*, the short story "The Magic Spinning Wheel" includes a character named for Smith's fictional heroine: "Her name was Ethelinde, and it was given to her by an aunt who had been reading the Recluse of the Lake, at the time just written by Mrs. Charlotte Smith, who had her nose put out of joint by the great Unknown, that everybody knows killed all his predecessors stone dead with a single flourish of his pen."[81] This "great Unknown" refers to Scott, who had been elected anonymously as "the author of Waverley" to the literary Roxburgh Club, making him "the great Unknown" to that society.[82] This gift book laments Smith's loss already in 1836 and lays the blame at the feet of Scott, reflecting a recognition of the importance of Scott's collection to the novel's history. The book foresees no chance for the revival of Smith and other of Scott's predecessors after being so dramatically deposed. It also introduces an everydayness to this knowledge—that Smith was forgotten and a reader would need a reminder of who she was and what she wrote and that Scott was the known destroyer of women novelists.

In 1862, Julia Kavanagh wrote in her *English Women of Letters* that Smith "had great talent—she was one of the best novelists of the day, but the haste and felicity with which she wrote, the gloom that overshadowed her life, robbed her of a durable literary fame." This acute observation acknowledges and perpetuates the Reviews' influence on Smith's legacy, even while Kavanagh herself could not help but comment on the "gloom" of Smith's life. "As a novelist she but helps to fill the vacant space between Miss Burney and Mrs. Radcliffe," Kavanagh proclaims, restoring the remembrance of the Reviews' sister-queen trio. But more specifically, Kavanagh's description of Smith's career is centered around Smith's "fall." "If we attempt to give Charlotte Smith her meed of praise in these pages," Kavanaugh laments, "it is not without the knowledge that she produced no strong impression, and will leave no lasting trace in the literature of the day."[83]

Kavanaugh's remembrance of Smith is still a forgetting—a forgetting of the late 1780s and early 1790s novels that were so well received, saw multiple editions, and stocked circulating libraries' shelves. The Reviews' public representation of Smith's fall is especially visible in Smith's first appearance in twentieth-century scholarly criticism. James R. Foster's article "Charlotte Smith, Pre-Romantic Novelist" (1928) privileges *Celestina*, noting that though "the greater part of Mrs. Smith's work was written after [*Celestina*] . . . often she 'fell' below her standard of achievement."[84] Foster offers an extensive reading of Smith's novels compared to those of Radcliffe but ends his article stating: "My purpose in balancing Ann Radcliffe's account book is not the rehabilitation of Charlotte Smith, for her works are dead, and justly so."[85]

Fortunately, scholars of the later twentieth century did not agree with Foster's insistence on the burial of Smith's works. The *NRD*'s data on Smith's rise and fall as a novelist and ability to track how the system of the Reviews criticized her and represented her to the English reading public as compared to her contemporaries helps us to uncover a richer understanding of Siskin's "Great Forgetting"—the why and how of once prolific and popular novelists disappearing from literary history and the novel's canon so suddenly. Filled out with a richness beyond that of a data point, the case of Smith tracks the long-reaching influence of the Reviews' representation of authors and of the novel. This gets at what Curran insisted was necessary for the next step in recovery work of Romantic women writers—"more of the actual records that give an individual cast to all of these writers as they function within a multitude of cultures."[86] Because the Reviews were incapable of accepting the novel's changing and varying forms that Smith's later prose pieces explore, her novel-writing career has been represented in our history of the genre as a rise-and-fall story, and indeed *that* is the history that the literary system of book reviewing had a hand in shaping. It is doubtful that such a simplified summary of her career could gain traction today, considering the heightened attention to nuance in Smith studies. It is, nevertheless, essential that when attempting to uncover the "real" Smith or continuing the sustained legacy of feminist literary history by giving greater attention to her works in their own right, we accurately recall where and how we inherited such a beleaguered author.

CHAPTER FOUR

A Study in 55 Novels

Data Trouble and Resistant Narratives in the Novel's History

Althea Fanshawe's *Easter Holidays, or Domestic Conversations, Designed for the Instruction, and it is hoped for the Amusement of Young People* (1797), published in Bath, was a combination of short fiction in dialogue and an almanac giving appropriate stories and meditations for the days around Easter Sunday. Fanshawe's introduction opens with an homage to her inspiration for writing: Charlotte Smith's *Rural Walks* (1795). Adopting the customary prefatory deference about her poor ability to write, Fanshawe claims: "although thoroughly conscious of not possessing the talents, which so eminently belong to the Writer of rural Walks; yet I must fairly acknowledge I was so much pleased with those Dialogues for the use of Children, that I resolved, at humble distance, in some degree to imitate them."[1] Smith notes in her *Rural Walks* that it was intended for "girls of twelve or thirteen" and that the work was partly her own tool for educating her daughters.[2] *Rural Walks* was popular, and Smith later published *Rambles Farther* (1796) and *Minor Morals* (1798) as continuations of her initial juvenile fiction success. *Easter Holidays* takes itself up as a companion to *Rural Walks*; its "conversations are offered particularly to Boys of the same age."[3] In *Easter Holidays*, Fanshawe follows in the footsteps of a well-respected novelist. Her preface even aligns with contemporary traditions outlined in Chapter 2: It anticipates criticism, requests leniency of the critics, discusses genre conventions, and expresses the author's intention for writing.[4] And though *Easter Holidays* is reviewed by the *Monthly* as a novel and is therefore part of the *Novels Reviewed Database, 1790–1820*, it is not included in Peter Garside, James Raven, and Rainer Schöwerling's *The English Novel 1770–1829*.[5] Nor is it in Andrew Block's *The English Novel, 1740–1850*.[6] It somehow does not *now* fit the definition of an eighteenth-century novel, but for the *Monthly Review*, and perhaps for Fanshawe, it did.

Fanshawe's work is not unique in this distinction. There are 55 novels recorded in the *NRD* that are missing from Garside, Raven, and Schöwerling's bibliography (see Appendix B). While I expected some data anomalies in creating the *NRD*, this number, 55, seemed surprisingly large to me, so I set out to consider these works carefully to better understand what they are and what they might, as a group and individually, teach us. A closer look at these 55 novels shows that they come from a range of alternate, sub-, or micro-genres (Table 4.1) that in the Romantic period were *sometimes* identified as novels but not consistently. Despite the Enlightenment's interest in collecting and classifying information, even by 1790, the novel's definition and parameters at times eluded the Reviewers. Additionally, each periodical's treatment of these individual works differed from one another—there was no consensus about what *exactly* made it difficult to definitively call them novels. Most were reviewed by only one of the Reviews. Of these 55 novels, 17 are reviewed by the *Monthly* alone, 28 by the *Critical* alone, and 10 by both Reviews. The *Critical* outpaces the *Monthly* in every subgenre reviewing category for these 55 novels, but this aligns with the *Critical*'s general practice of reviewing more novels than the *Monthly*—the *Monthly* features 761 reviews of novels from 1790 to 1820, while the *Critical* boasts 967.

While both journals review many of the juvenile and didactic works from this list, the *Critical* gives far more attention to translations, collections of short stories, abridgments, and dialogues than the *Monthly*. Only 18 percent of the works on this list are noticed by both Reviews, whereas overall in the *NRD*, 25 percent of novels tracked are reviewed in both publications. This lower percentage perhaps suggests that these outliers indicate something about the individual reviewers' attitudes toward the opaque boundaries of the novel's genre. How each periodical treats the various subgenres in this dataset may also suggest to us something about their genre understandings or reviewing practices. Regardless, this lack of consistency across the reviewing system of these 55 novels reminds us that it is an *active* system that, when placed against the rigidity of

Subgenres of 55 Novels

Subgenre	Translation	Juvenile Fiction	Didactic	Memoir/ True Life	From a Real MSS	Ancient Text Translation	Short Stories	Adaptation/ Abridgment	Dialogue
Total Works	16	25	26	3	2	4	20	4	8
Monthly Review	7	12	13	2	0	2	9	1	3
Critical Review	12	16	18	2	2	3	13	3	6
Both	3	3	5	0	0	1	2	0	1

modern data-collection practices, will inevitably turn up resistant items—items that resist some or all attempts to classify or organize them.

I began attending to these 55 resistant novels by attempting to understand them under areas of scrutiny relevant to the *NRD*. My findings highlight some of the genre boundaries that modern scholars place upon novels from this period in addition to those our eighteenth-century predecessors grappled with. I surmised that some of the works in this dataset may have been reviewed as novels based on their authorship. For example, the *Critical Review* praises Charles Lamb's *Tales from Shakespeare, designed for the Use of young Persons* (1807), perhaps because a few years earlier, they had reviewed his *A Tale of Rosamund Gray and Old Blind Margaret* (1798).[7] Lamb's other work in this list, *Felissa; or the Life and Opinions of a Kitten of Sentiment* (1811), features colored engravings of said kitten, so the *Critical*'s review devotes a page and a half to summarizing the puss's adventures, declaring that "our Juvenile readers" will welcome the work, giving it "a conspicuous place in their library."[8] Other well-known novelists in the cohort include Mary Hays, best known for her *Memoirs of Emma Courtney* (1796), which was reviewed by both periodicals, and Mary Pilkington, who published over 40 novels in addition to children's literature.

Forty of the works in this dataset are published in only one volume, so their short length might also contribute to their nebulous genre identification. Both *Paternal Love; or, The Reward of Friendship* (1815) by Peter Middleton Darling and Maria Susanna Cooper's *The Wife* (1813) are cited in Garside, Raven, and Schöwerling's appendix as "Uncertain reconstituted/unseen titles." The note for Cooper's work cites its absence from contemporary circulating catalogue lists of novels and the fact that it "is a work directed at children" as further reasons to exclude it from their bibliography, while Darling's, though listed in New-man's Minerva Library Catalogue, is referred to as "possibly a short tale." *The British Fiction Database* revisits the genre possibilities of *Paternal Love* in their Update 4, citing the *Monthly*'s review as "new evidence [that] strengthens the claim for this work to be included in the main listings" while noting that "some uncertainty about its length and whether or not a juvenile audience is targeted remain."[9] Audience and length of a work, then, are factors that modern scholars consider when outlining generic parameters of the late eighteenth- and early nineteenth-century novel that might conflict with contemporary genre understandings. Neither of these boundaries are necessarily erroneous, but they are important to know when using these various bibliographies as tools for our study of the period.

The subgenres featured in this list are also revealing (Table 4.1). Almost half of the novels in this dataset fall under two categories, which I have called juvenile fiction and didactic fiction. Here juvenile fiction is any work that declares itself in title or preface as written for children or adolescents. Didactic fiction is any work that declares in title or preface, or through direct moralizing in chapter or story titles, that it intends to teach readers a lesson. Each of these 55 novels fall under multiple categories (e.g., 18 are both juvenile fiction and didactic fiction—two subcategories that naturally intersect).[10] Twenty are collections of shorter stories. Four are abridgments aimed at bringing longer or more complex texts to new audiences. Sixteen are translations of a work from a language other than English, four of which are translations of ancient or classic works.[11] Two that claim to be taken from old manuscripts, a common novel-writing trope, can actually be identified as related to a real manuscript,[12] and three can be connected to actual memoirs of the individual they claim to biographize/autobiographize, despite the title of "Memoir" also operating largely as a fictional frame structure in this period.[13] For three of the works there are no known extant copies, and their scant reviews are hardly enough to support any arguments about their style, other than that they are reviewed as novels. These are *Theodore and Blanche; or the Victims of Love* (1808) by Sophie Ristaud Cotton, *Paternal Love; or, the Reward of Friendship* by Darling, and *Rosa; or, Village Incidents* (1817), whose author is currently unknown.[14] The lack of extant copies of these works has likely instigated their exclusion from modern bibliographies.

It is telling that genres that largely focused on domestic elements, like educating children, or that were associated with women, such as translations, are prevalent here. They have, at some point, been judged by modern scholars to be outside the generic boundaries of the novel. How modern scholars may otherwise classify, generically, these 55 novels centers around biases that overwhelmingly perpetuate the marginalization of women writers and continually othered voices in our scholarship about the English novel. Further, it is likely that said biases about the borders of the novel's genre are established or maintained through these works' exclusion from foundational reference texts.

Garside, Raven, and Schöwerling's methodology helps illuminate the genesis of these 55 novels' genre resistance or, perhaps more specifically, what parameters scholars of the novel have been working under that they resist. The subtitle of the bibliography, *a Survey of Prose Fiction*, declares an express concern with *genre.* The scope of any reference text is the prerogative of the scholar(s) and one of the important reasons why we must understand bibliography as a scholarly practice informed by the judgment and background of its compilers.[15]

The editors point to why bibliographical scholarship on the English novel matters and what their bibliography intends to do: "Identify authorship, communities of writing, the themes embraced and repeated by writers, the circumstances of novel production, and the nature of literary circulation and reception."[16] In explaining their scope and selection parameters, the editors note that "no bibliography of this kind can escape difficult editorial decisions over inclusion and exclusion."[17] This is true, and such an ambitious project is likely to have human and historically contributed errors. And, though the study "includes what contemporaries thought of as novels" and their data-collection methodology "incorporate[s] works categorized as 'novels' in contemporary periodical reviews," this large number of novels, 55, resist the study's genre constraints yet show up in the *NRD*.[18]

Some of their intentional genre exclusions speak to how we understood the novel at the time of the study. For example, they "exclud[e] religious tracts, chapbooks, literature written only for children and juveniles, and very short separately issued tales." They also list verse novels as an omission. These exclusions partly explain why Fanshawe's work shows up in the 55 novels cohort. Acknowledging that the broad genre of the novel was still in flux and contested across the period of their study, the editors also admit that "books which do not now appear to us to be novels were then reviewed under this category." Some texts were still difficult for the editors to classify; for example, they wrestled with the parameters for the exclusion of juvenile fiction: "In a very few instances [three], where a work evidently enjoyed a wider currency, an exception has been made."[19] What might a "wider currency" include? Are circulation, reception, and literary value (whose? the Reviews?) invisible "currency"? Is "wider currency" a way to think about the fluctuating understanding of genre during this period? Might some of these 55 novels fit under this umbrella? What stands out to me is that all of these areas the bibliography lists in its original aim—authorship, communities, themes, reception, circumstances of writing or disseminating prose fiction—are also influenced by authorial gender.

As it is the main scope of *this* book, gender is central to the case studies I pull from this list of 55 novels to consider in further detail here. Though my overall dataset in the *NRD* is significantly smaller in number and scope than all that *The English Novel, 1770–1829* collated, I turn to it with as much scrutiny because I value what it might teach me. So, in examining these 55 novels, I consider the problem with data-driven and quantitative studies that Lauren Klein identifies where gender, sexuality, and race are concerned—"problems associated with scale." Klein notes that these problems "require increased attention to, rather than a passing over" of small pockets of data that are "occluded when taking a distant view." She gives the following questions to ask of our data: "What might be hidden in this corpus? Are there methods we might use to bring out [things] that the eye cannot see?" It is the elements that resist our models that we should attend to, argues Klein, "lest we inadvertently reinscribe the same power relations that we intend to critique" back upon our data—and that is what this chapter attempts to do.[20]

It is no coincidence then that attending to works and people which resist our methods of study is also the argument Margaret Ezell makes in *Writing Women's Literary History*.[21] Women are the largest group of peoples disenfranchised by academic methodologies informed by centuries of patriarchal measures of value and success.[22] Further marginalized peoples within this demographic have been more than neglected; they have been maligned. Scholarly assumptions about the absence of marginalized peoples in history, and therefore in our data and research methodologies, are compounded for individuals with intersectional identities—that is, those who live under the marginalization of gender and also with oppressed identities relating to class, sexuality, race, ability, nationality, and age.[23] As Imtiaz Habib argues, "what is little looked for, and what is therefore non-existent, is also what is/should be unknown because it cannot be known. This in turn reinforces the conventional contemporary mistruth" of that unknown group's assumed complete absence from a period of time, a subject of study, or the history of a genre.[24]

Assumptions of absence in our bibliographies of the English novel precede scholars' failure to look for multiply marginalized novelists and learn about them in data-driven work. And further, a failure to speak directly about how these peoples are or are not represented in our bibliographies and data-collection methodologies *is itself* an act of the assumption of absence. These multiply marginalized novelists are the focus of this chapter, and I discuss how my identification of them came from a way that the *NRD* "troubles" other bibliographies in the field. As my work stands in critique, it also invites future scholars to ask their own questions about my findings.[25]

It is my hope that this study will illuminate these writers and the genre assumptions that placed them in this cohort so that we might consider them as signposts for future work and be aware that all datasets likely include similar silenced pockets that warrant in-depth investigation. In the two case studies considered here, which follow the authorship, writing and publication, biographical context, and contemporary reception of the works at hand, I let authorial gender center how I might better understand the resistant texts. I investigated who these writers were, how their identities informed their writing, and how that writing might be at odds with modern genre boundaries. I show that the contributions of a woman with disabilities, Fanshawe, and a queer woman, Ethelinda Potts, are either removed from our datasets, bibliographies, and literary histories when we discard resistant data or are silenced when we do not attend to it. These case studies are not exhaustive; there is much to their stories that cannot be told in the space I have here, and there are other cases from the 55-novel cohort that warrant further investigation. I point to these two because they showcase texts that frustrate current genre boundaries *and* feature authorships by people with intersectional identities, making them multiply marginalized in the history of the novel. I hope to show here that a history of the novel that includes these contributors is richer, more robust, and more just in its equitable acknowledgment of the authors of the genre and reveals the rewards of sitting with our resistant data.

Case Study 1: Althea Fanshawe, Children's Literature, and Writers with Disabilities

Althea Fanshawe (1759–1824) was 38 years old in 1797 when she published her *Easter Holidays*, included in the 55-novel cohort.[26] It is, as far as I can tell, her first foray into print publication. Many of Fanshawe's published works could be classified as miscellanies, almanacs, devotionals, or educational texts as well as fictional narratives in prose form—novels. In addition to *Easter Holidays*, Fanshawe authored *Thoughts on affectation: addressed chiefly to young people* (1805), *Sunday Reflections* (1809), *Occasional considerations on various passages of Scripture* (1812), and possibly other shorter religious works that claim a chain of authorship back to *Thoughts on affectation*.[27] These texts were concerned with the ways that daily life, morality, education, spirituality, and storytelling intersected. These same intersections might also be used to describe other canonical novels, such as the labors and sermonizing of Daniel Defoe's *Robinson Crusoe*, the letters and reflections of Samuel Richardson's *Clarissa*, or the ins and outs of London daily life in Frances Burney's *Evelina*. But Fanshawe's works stand out from these in their direct address to and interest in adolescent and juvenile readers.

The didactic nature of many novels from this period complicates our understanding of why a text like *Easter Holidays* might have been excluded from modern novel bibliographies, though it was reviewed contemporarily as a novel. *Easter Holidays*, one would think, should have a similar experience in the reviewing system to its inspiration text by Smith, *Rural Walks*, but this is not the case. Smith declares in her introduction to *Rural Walks* that she "wished to unite the interest of the novel with the instruction of the school-book," and she used dialogues to bridge that gap.[28] *Rural Walks*, however, was not reviewed as a novel, despite the preface's claims. It was reviewed in the *Monthly Review*'s Monthly Catalogue section titled "Education."[29] Relegating Smith's publications to the Monthly Catalogue at this point in the 1790s was consistent with how the *Monthly* was responding to Smith's novels, as outlined in Chapter 3.

The *Critical*, however, recognized *Rural Walks* in its front section, granting the work almost four pages of space, but does not call it a novel.[30] Of the *Critical*'s review, three and a half pages are excerpts from Smith's preface and of a later section that features two of the original sonnets Smith includes in the volume. It is notable that the *Critical* quotes Smith's preface on writing *Rural Walks* "in the very little time that the incessant necessity of writing for the support of [her] family allows [her] to bestow on the education" of her daughters— keeping with their practice of drawing attention to Smith's politics and personal life in their criticisms of her work though continuing to feature it in the front of their periodical.[31] The *Monthly*'s piece, focused almost entirely on Smith's preface, illustrates an interest in the intentions and plans for a work that combines the novel and schoolbooks but does not review it as a novel.

It is unclear why *Easter Holidays*, which follows Smith's plan to present a combination of educational text and novel, is, unlike *Rural Walks* itself, reviewed by the *Monthly* under the "Novels" section of their Monthly Catalogue in June of 1798. Perhaps *Easter Holidays* fulfilled this intention better than Smith's original. Fanshawe's *Easter Holidays* received more summary and evaluation by the *Monthly* than *Rural Walks*. The work appeared to meet the Reviews' requirement to be original and keep a reader interested—"the volume being divided into days and particular occurrences, the tedium attending a continual narration is happily avoided."[32] After two-thirds of a page of summary and review criticism, the *Monthly* excerpts a lengthy section in verse, taking up one and a quarter pages of their Monthly Catalogue. This excerpt of verse from the largely prose work parallels the *Monthly*'s excerpt of Smith's original poetry from *Rural Walks*.

Alternately, the *Critical* recognizes *Easter Holidays* in the "Education" section of their October 1799 Monthly Catalogue with a favorable critique. Their review notes that "this work was first suggested by the perusal of *Rural Walks*," drawing out the connection between Fanshawe and Smith's texts.[33] Though a positive review, it takes up less than a quarter of the page. It is important to note that the Reviews were not always consistent in their reviewing practices or generic distinctions across the period of this study. As a literary system rather than a stagnant reference source, the Reviews represent "the complex history by which those artifacts and phenomena are transmitted to and by us in the present."[34] Modern scholars who hope to come to the Reviews for concrete, consistent, unbiased facts about literary history will be sorely disappointed and wholly misunderstand *living* historical systems. The Reviews are a living representation of an interaction between literary critics, the literary readership of the day, the politics of the book market, and many other contributing factors. It is understandable, then, that they might represent two similar works differently, as they do with Smith and Fanshawe.

The treatment of *Easter Holidays* in both the *Monthly* and the *Critical* calls attention to an issue mentioned in "The Procedure for and Guide to Using *The Novels Reviewed Database, 1790–1820*": By adhering to the practices of a historical literary system, some events that modern scholars might call "inconsistencies" emerge.[35] Some works are reviewed in one periodical and not the other or are reviewed as a novel in only one and recognized as part of different generic conventions by the other. Perhaps *Easter Holidays* is reviewed as a novel due to its connection to Smith, or perhaps the genre-bending nature of the work itself or differing understandings of the genre by critics or audiences explain its inclusion in the Review pages. Regardless, the inclusion of *Easter Holidays* in the cohort of 55 novels begs us to learn more about it and the kinds of works and writers that would otherwise lay uncelebrated without a closer look at our data outliers. An exploration of how *Easter Holidays* fits into the subgenre traditions of its time and the ways that its author, Fanshawe, wrote it while experiencing periods of immobility as a result of her chronic illness and disability can reveal how resistant texts are often tied to marginalized peoples. Perhaps it ought to be unsurprising that the writings of authors who lived within a realm of otherness resist conformity to our generic understandings.

As juvenile fiction, Fanshawe's *Easter Holidays* participated in an already circulating conversation between 1760 and 1845 regarding whether children should be educated at home or sent away to school. Though sending children to school was an economical option for working-class families, disciples of Jean-Jacques Rousseau's *Emile* (1762) increasingly wrote on the merits of each. The consensus of children's literature in general was that children learn best with other children and that a combination of formal school (boarding or day schools) and daily, organic in-home education, often overseen by a mother or relative, was best. M. O. Grenby follows the "links between domestic education and the children's literature of the period," pointing specifically to "publishers and authors [who] presented children's books as having derived from the home and as fit to be used there" for educational purposes.[36] Grenby's extensive research on children's literature also highlights that "novelists, and children's novelists in particular, discussed the issue as a perennially unsettled question."[37] Many well-established novelists wrote prose fiction intended for the education of younger readers. Anna Laetitia Barbauld, Mary Wollstonecraft, Hannah More, Maria Edgeworth, and Smith used their experience overseeing juvenile education to write novels for a wider readership.

Easter Holidays serves to bridge the domestic and private/formal education of its characters and considers how to guide parents in continuing and supporting their children's education when they were home from formal schooling. When *Easter Holidays* was published in 1797, some of Fanshawe's nephews, her brother Henry Fanshawe's younger children, were of the age she was writing for: William, aged 13; Frederick, aged 9; and George, aged 8. Though Fanshawe never married nor had children, she had a close relationship with her five nephews, corresponding with them often when they were not visiting her. During this period, "the rise of children's literature led to a tremendous surge in female literary production," although there was also probably a lot of literature written for these audiences that was not published because it was rather quickly put to use in homes or schools without being formally printed.[38]

Fanshawe, whose formal education we know little about but whose intellect and interest in her nephews we cannot doubt, entered this movement of women using hybrid prose genres for younger readers as a foray into professional publishing. Grenby divides children's literature into subgenera, citing that "the author's gender was seldom the only and certainly not the principal, factor in the ascription of value to a work" by a publisher. He later concedes that value *was* influenced by circumstances determined by gender, noting that "in the book trade as a whole, the generic boundaries of children's publishing were carefully controlled. It was, in practical terms, difficult for women to break into the higher-status, higher-earning categories" like anthologies, instructional works, and religious works but not into those of stories and tales.[39] Like Smith's *Rural Walks, Easter Holidays* straddles two genres, and this may have been intentional, given the traditions and boundaries to publication in children's literature. Fanshawe's presence in this cohort of 55 novels illustrates a generic integration we should be aware of when considering the way that the history of the English novel has been conceived of, written about, and understood by scholars: the treatment of juvenile audiences as an important factor for defining the novel's boundaries.

Easter Holidays also points to a type of *author* who is scorned or indeed wiped from lists entirely as a result of genre boundaries defined in our earliest scholarship by elite, nondisabled, cisgendered, heterosexual male scholars. Fanshawe was one of three surviving children of Althea Fanshawe (née Snelling) and Simon Fanshawe. She came from a family of writers. Her ancestor, Sir Richard Fanshawe (1608–1666), published several works of translation during his lifetime. Fanshawe's mother had a manuscript copy of the writings of Sir Richard's wife, the Lady Ann Fanshawe (1625–1680), *The Memoirs of Lady Anne Fanshawe*. Many women in the family copied the memoirs over for familial use, including our author, whose 1790s manuscript was used as the copy text for the work's first printing in 1830.[40]

Lady Ann Fanshawe's household book, *Mrs. Fanshawe's Book of Receipts and Physickes, Wasters, Cordialls, Preserves, and Cookery* (1651) is also held in manuscript at the Wellcome Library.[41] Making detailed records of a woman's life and knowledge and of a household's comings and goings was a tradition that Fanshawe knew well and may have influenced her interest in children's education in the home. Fanshawe's will proclaims her a "spinster," and the family histories written by later generations tend to gloss over not only her accomplishments but her very existence.[42] The longest notice given in *The History of the Fanshawe Family* (1927) to her is by her descendant H. C. Fanshawe (1852–1923), who characterizes her life as one "of constant suffering, most bravely borne to its close," and says that in spite of her illness, "she continued to take an interest in everything round her, wrote verses in her earlier years (as all young ladies did then), and religious books which commanded wide notice, in her middle life."[43] H. C. Fanshawe's notice of the author's chronic illness is confirmed by the writer herself in her later *Thoughts on Affectation* (1805): "Whether I shall have succeeded in serving or amusing any one of my readers, I know not; but I have amused and so far served myself, that I have employed many a lonely hour in the chamber of sickness, which might have been gloomy, had it not been filled by writing the trifle, which I now submit to a less partial judgement than that of its author."[44] Fanshawe likely had epilepsy, along with chronic bouts of rheumatism and gout. Though there are few records from Fanshawe's early life, as an adult she recorded the details of her intellectual interests, physical health, relationships to her family and friends, and connections to and opinions about the wider world in a diary she kept after the death of her mother in 1805 until February 1824, just two months before her own death. During this period, she lived in Bath near the Royal Crescent, likely to receive medical treatment.

By examining Fanshawe's publications and life as she recorded it, we can better attend to how she and writers like her are active though neglected authors of the English novel. Data gathered from a title page generally cannot count disability, so we can and should understand datasets to be inherently ableist unless otherwise expanded on in collection methodologies. It is also essential to understand that our very genre parameters may be ableist themselves. Assuming an author is not disabled or using *only* genre values created, circulated, and enforced by ableist structures like the patriarchy or the literary system of book reviewing perpetuates ableism in our scholarship. Fanshawe's case shows us that though the *NRD*'s construction methodology enables us to capture people with disabilities in our data, it also threatens to obscure or erase them if resistant data is disregarded. In order to make this one data point from the *NRD* more expansive, it is necessary to add supplemental primary sources, namely Fanshawe's diary, to our study of her *Easter Holidays*. I herein examine Fanshawe's diary as a necessity to underpin a contextual reading of *Easter Holidays* that illuminates how an ableist refusal to read disability texts on their own terms starves our datasets, and thereby our histories, of the richness of disability-informed worldviews, experiences, and lives.

Fanshawe's uncatalogued and unpublished diary is held at Valence House Museum in Dagenham, London, with her family's papers. Its organization reveals her conception of how her life and disability fit into the wider world. The diary is divided into four sections for each year: (1) "family events and circumstances relative to myself"; (2) "family marriages, deaths, or births"; (3) "marriages, deaths, or births amongst acquaintances or neighbors"; and (4) "events private and public." These distinctions reflect Fanshawe's understanding of how she was divided from, yet living alongside, the nondisabled persons in her circle and in the public at large. The "private" differ from "family events" in that they are largely still public information (e.g., inheritances, travel). The fourth section is divided into two and is on facing pages with the "events private" on the verso and the word "public" on the recto facing page. The "public" events record parliamentary votes, public scandals, celebrity births/deaths, decisions about the Regency, battles, grain shortage riots, and the goings-on of the Royal family, with special attention paid to illnesses. Each month is listed in a column on the left of each section, and the events that fall under that month are written out beside it (Figure 4.1).

The monthly parallel format across these sections shows Fanshawe was acutely aware of the ebb and flow of her health and mobility. The fact that she tracked the health of her own family along with newspaper reports of King George III's neurological disability provides an excellent example of the lived

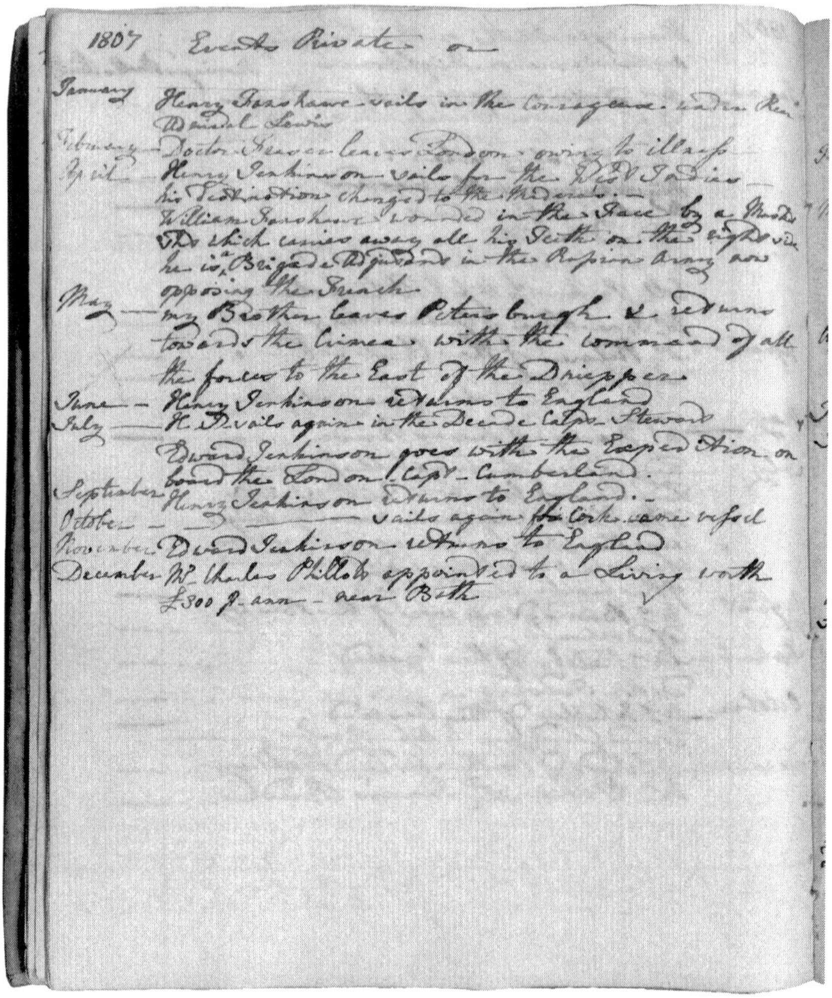

Figure 4.1a, 4.1b. (*above and opposite*) Double page spread from Althea Fanshawe's diary 1807 showing "Events Private or" on the verso, or left side, and "Public" on the rector, or right side. The events are divided by a vertical column labeling each month. Valence House Museum.

February — Buenos Ayres retaken by the Spaniards
Victory of the Russians over the French — This is a
more bloody action, after which both the Armies
claim the Victory?
abolition of the Slave Trade

March — Trial of S[i]r Home Popham for having acted contrary
to orders when he took Buenos Ayres, — acquitted
of positive guilt, but severely reprimanded?!
Complete change of Ministry — Duke of Portland
now at the Head

April — Capture of Monte Video by S[i]r S. Auchmuty & Adm[iral]
Stirling
Dissolution of Parliament

June — Meeting of the New Parliament

July — Decided Victory of the French over the Russians
which produces an immediate Armistice asked
for by the defeated party
Duchess of Brunswick comes to reside in England
Peace concluded between Russia Prussia and
France

August — Death of the Duchess of Gloucester.—

September — Defeat of English Troops in South America.
forced to give up Monte Video & to move from
the Rio de la Plata with a loss of upwards of
1100 men. — S[i]r S. Auchmuty & Gen[eral] Crawford return
to England
Surrender of Copenhagen & of the whole Danish
Fleet to the British forces under Admiral Gambier
& Lord Cathcart.—

October — return to England.—

November — strange arrival of Lewis 18th in England.

December — Russia declares Enmity — War determined upon
Departure of the Portuguese Royal Family for
South America under English protection.—

experience and understanding of chronic illness and invisible disability by a woman of means in the period. Fanshawe recorded events relating to her health—bouts of illness, "fits," medical treatments, and her physical mobility—in her diary's "family events and circumstances relative to myself" section. It is notable that she differentiated familial events from those in the "private" pages of the "events private and public" section; Fanshawe suggests that the changes in medicine dosing or stints of immobility were relative to her alone. The end of each year in Fanshawe's diary is marked with totals for the two forms her chronic illness took: "fits" and "attacks." It is not clear how she discerned the two—both seem to be related to her epilepsy. Between 1805 and 1823, Fanshawe documented an average of 35 "fits" and 131 "attacks" per year.[45]

Fanshawe, like most individuals with chronic and invisible illness, was "well" or seemingly able-bodied until she was not. Multiple entries in her diary note Fanshawe walking out in the Royal Crescent, an ostensibly benign activity but one not taken for granted by a person whose mobility was transitory. Fanshawe's records of walking outside are often indications of the first time she was able to do so following confinement from a period of illness. And though these moments are recorded precisely because they contrast with the previous period of inactivity (e.g., on April 2, 1819: "After confinement since last October walk out for half an hour in the Crescent"), they also indicate that Fanshawe regularly walked about the Crescent (or tried to) for exercise or pleasure.[46] Travis Chi Wang Lau asserts that an "ongoing problem in disability studies since its emergence in the 1980s [is] the marginalization of invisible disabilities and chronic illness," and Fanshawe's case is no different.[47] Fanshawe's life oscillates between periods of chronic invisible illness and times when her disabilities become visually evident to those around her, such as when she uses a wheelchair to get some air in the Crescent.

Fanshawe's "fits and attacks" often robbed her of her physical mobility and obliged her to stay indoors. On occasion, she had these "fits" while out in public and had to be transported home. On October 2, 1812, she was "seized with a fit in the gravel walk and brought home in a chair." On September 13, 1813, she was "taken with a fit when walking in Marlborough Buildings." And on September 12, 1816, she was "taken with a bad fit when walking in the Crescent & carried to Mrs. Danbury's house."[48] The family historian H. C. Fanshawe added to Althea Fanshawe's diary in his hand at the end of the entries for 1816 that

> Miss Penelope S recorded in her journal of Nov 1816 that she visited Ms A Fanshawe "a sad monument of the afflicting tho' not destructive (!) effects of epi-

lepsy. She has been for 22 years a confined invalid seeing but few relations & Mr
& Mrs Bowlles. Considering the life she leads it is astonishing that her facilities
are not more impaired for she is able to employ All her time in reading writing
and work. Her only defect is from the wont of communication with others, which
throws her back entirely on herself & her few concerns, & renders her open to
small prejudices & too little able vary the source of her ideas with what is passing
around her" [note added now, 1915].[49]

H. C. Fanshawe provides no citations for this later-added reflection on Fanshawe's neurological disability by a supposed contemporary, but it does reveal
the degree to which Fanshawe was removed from general company due to her
disability. Miss Penelope S reveals her prejudice where Fanshawe's disability is
concerned when she asserts that "it is astonishing that [Fanshawe's] facilities
are not more impaired" and that "she is able to employ all her time in reading
writing and work." Fanshawe lived in a world that not only did not welcome or
support her disability and bodymind, but actively shunned her for it. Margaret
Price uses the term "bodymind" to indicate the interconnectedness of the body
and the mind, especially in the lives of folks with disabilities, and it is particularly relevant to Fanshawe's life as an author.[50] Her interest in the health of other
public figures like King George III and later Queen Caroline in her diary's
"Events Private and Public" sections shows Fanshawe observing the "public"
world not wholly as an outsider but rather tracking the ways that she fit into it
or that the world at large reported on, ridiculed, or at times *did* make space for
people with disabilities. Fanshawe's records of agreeing on publication terms,
correcting proofs, and returning them to the press alongside notations doc-
umenting her disability are a narrative of her authorship in "crip time"—the
molding of time to fit the body, rather than the body to fit a (presumed)
able-bodied time.[51] The diary unfolds in the ebb and flow of events and pace of
life through Fanshawe's crip time and maps it onto the rhythms of crip time oc-
cupied by public figures, relatives with disability—often temporary due to illness or injury—and other more universal time stamps of life: births, marriages,
deaths.

Fanshawe's life positioned her as a keen observer of the relationships, movements, and social interactions of people around her, and her first publication
addresses the subjects her diary would later consider. *Easter Holidays'* structure
meditates on time, family, mobility, education, and storytelling. In each chapter, the young men are home from school, often outdoors, taking their lessons
while on walks. Fanshawe enters the contemporary printed discussion about

juvenile education through a story grounded in domestic mobility. Without the personal experience of an education away from home at a boy's school, Fanshawe contributes instead to the ways that engaging with the natural world, even in a localized way, is itself a rich education and centers learning on human interaction and the novelistic telling of the stories of everyday life. If Miss Penelope S's assertion about Fanshawe being confined for 22 years by 1816 is an accurate assessment of how long she had been withdrawn from most public life, then at the publication of *Easter Holidays* in 1797, she was already living and cultivating a self-understanding of her bodymind and crip time against the intellectual and physical development of her active nephews. Without the context of Fanshawe's diary, the privileges of daily walks and chatter with visiting neighbors in *Easter Holidays* might easily be dismissed as commonplace rather than as cultivated and desirous learning environments that Fanshawe crafts mindfully for her readers.

Fanshawe turns more pointedly to writing about disability in her next publication, and in it, she reflects on the differing worldviews held by people who experience disability and those who are currently able-bodied. It is a book that offers commentary on personalities and social standards from a disability perspective. In *Thoughts on Affectation* (1805), Fanshawe describes the various attributes displayed by her contemporaries and how their real or "affected" characteristics relate to the human condition. Following the sections on "Amiable Qualifications" and "Disagreeable Habits" is the final section, "Accidental Circumstances of Life, not depending on ourselves." This section includes general topics like Beauty, Youth, Ugliness, Age, and Poverty but also more specific physical "Circumstances" related to disability and aligning with Fanshawe's own life: Bodily Strength, Good Health, Weakness, and Illness. Fanshawe observes, "Natural, constitutional Good Health is so entirely out of our reach, that to affect it is as ridiculous, indeed as fruitless, as it would be for a dwarf to emulate the height of a giant."[52] She criticizes individuals who do not take care of their health and whose experiences with an unwell state are due to their own carelessness about their bodies.

Fanshawe's diary does not indicate the degree to which she shared the details of her chronic illness and disability with her family, but she observes in *Thoughts* that often the loved ones of the chronically ill are "no longer alarmed for the fate of the sick person." This, she argues, is because they have "often overcome similar attacks," and she notes that while this "sort of indifference" does not indicate a lack of compassion, it "is the natural effect of a natural cause—the certain operation of time."[53] By this, she means able-bodied time. This reflection might explain Fanshawe's including entries about her health under her diary section as "relevant to myself" but not to others and why she used her mounting observations of people and activities to populate the energetic schedule of the young in *Easter Holidays.*

Whether or not Fanshawe's family knew the intimate details of her physical health, they did attend upon her diligently in visits and correspondence and consulted her on all kinds of daily and milestone life matters. This may be because upon the death of her mother (and namesake), Fanshawe became, for all intents and purposes, the head of the family. She inherited significant monies and properties from her mother's family, both through her mother and directly from her maternal aunt, Anna Snelling. Althea the elder and Althea the younger both willed their properties, investments, and finances away from their son/brother, Henry, naming Henry's second son, the Reverend Charles Robert Fanshawe (1780–1859), and his children after him their heirs.[54] The Fanshawe family was one in which the women regularly looked out for one another in their wills, specifically leaving finances and property to other women in the family.[55] This tradition of ensuring female welfare is what made Fanshawe's life as an unmarried woman with a disability one of some independence. Fanshawe's financial freedom bought her extensive medical care and a house in Bath, servants to run her home, and the requirement that her relations never neglect her attentions because of her position holding the familial purse strings. It also, therefore, gave her the leisure and funds to pursue a life of the mind as a writer and to keep up with literary topics.

Easter Holidays is about being young, healthy, and active, having access to education and an easy, happy family life—all things denied to Fanshawe because of her disabilities. Its experimental form, combining an almanac parallel to Fanshawe's own diary, dialogues that take the place of visitors she so desperately desired, an education she was denied, and representing characters in robust health that she did not enjoy, showcases fiction as a space where Fanshawe could participate in and imagine a different life for herself. Perhaps *Easter Holidays* is a wish for Fanshawe, or perhaps it is an indicator of the many ways that ableist prejudices reach far beyond accessibility in physical form—but in fictional forms as well.

Fanshawe made space for her voice in a subgenre that many modern scholars fail to value: works for children. Like children, persons with disabilities in the eighteenth century were deemed either not intellectual or developed enough, not grown or "human" enough, or not advanced enough in creative contributions to meet "value" (or genre) parameters that (by their assumption of nondisability) were inherently ableist. Yet, the literary system of book reviewing provided multiple opportunities for genre variation to enter the contemporary critical conversation about and attempts to define the English novel. In turn, the sporadic inclusion of prose fiction for young readers in the reviewing system is indicative of the shifting or fluid boundaries of the genre. Perhaps a move away from rigid data-collection methodologies, which I admittedly adhered to in creating the *NRD*, would, like the reviewing system, offer up more such avenues for divergent authors and narratives to enter our literary history. In those cases, it might be easier for authors like Fanshawe, whose reflections on education, bodily autonomy, health, domesticity, family, and intellectual pursuits were personal for her storytelling, to challenge us to evaluate other ableist constraints we continue to place on the novel.

Case Study 2: Ethelinda Potts, Queer Writers, and Genre Bending

The anonymously published *Moonshine, a Novel* (1814) was reviewed with the following curt pronouncement in the March 1815 issue of the *Critical Review*: "The sickly offspring of a sickly bed. We wish the author better health." This quip responds to the work's address "To The Stranger" (preceding its preface), which claims that the "project" is the "employment [of] an invalid."[56] Like Fanshawe, its author took to the page when not of vigorous health. This text in the cohort of 55 novels is the most generically deviant. *Moonshine* is a collection of miscellaneous verse, although several of the poems are about novel reading and writing or discuss criticism and authorship in general. The *Monthly* reviews the volumes under the "Poetry" heading of their Monthly Catalogue of November the previous year and perhaps more correctly describes the work as "the emptying of a Commonplace-Book."[57] This assessment is perhaps in response to one of the pieces in *Moonshine*'s poetical preface, titled "On My Writing In My Son's Ciphering Book, But Half Filled, When He Began Mathematics," revealing that the author is writing wherever they can find the space.[58] The *Critical* inserts the genre marker of "a novel" in their review, though the work's title page reads only *Moonshine*. The *Universal Magazine*, *The New Monthly Magazine and Universal Register*, the *Edinburgh Annual Register*, *The Edinburgh Review*, and *The Monthly Museum* all include *Moonshine* in their New Publications lists under the heading of "Poetry."

How, then, did *Moonshine* find itself reviewed as a novel in the 1814 *Critical Review*? Perhaps the title sounded novelesque. There was a fashion for single-word novel titles consisting of a common noun.[59] *Moonshine* aligned with titles like *Home* (1802), *Casualties* (1804), *Self-Controul* (1811), and *Discipline* (1814).

Single-word titles followed by a generic descriptor like "a tale" or "a history" were even more common and may explain the *Critical* attaching the phrase "a novel" to the work's title in their review.[60] The reviewer may even have submitted their few lines without reading past the preface in order to complete their work quota.[61] If it was a mere slip-up of a busy reviewer, then, why might it be fruitful to pursue a history of this text and its authorship here? By tracing the authorial biography, publication history, and social and financial pressures that influenced both, I found that *Moonshine* highlights exactly who and what circumstances we silence when we try to occlude the untidy parts of our data.

Moonshine, its author, and their story are part of the period's literary history, though one not often or easily given voice, and I provide extensive detail here so that future scholars may pursue more advanced and thorough work on it/ them. The published work of a queer woman estranged from her family, *Moonshine* represents her attempt to reconnect with her children. It is one way that its author, Ethelinda Margaretta Potts, [62] could write her own family, life, love, and *truth* into the world. As she was a queer woman in the eighteenth century, it should perhaps be unsurprising that genre bending was what best suited the telling of her experience. What *Moonshine* is and does, then, can only be understood through a thorough resurrection of her background and family life.

Ethelinda would go on to publish a series of volumes under the title of *Moonshine* that might be considered revisions of that work, sequels, or new works altogether. They generally resist our bibliographical parameters for editions. These works regularly refer to her relationship with her children and provide evidence of her life estranged from her husband and the new life that she built with her partner, Sarah (Sally) Langford. I herein give a background of Ethelinda's legal tangle with her husband, followed by a bibliographical account of her *Moonshine* publications and their reflections of her motherhood. Finally, I explore how, as a queer woman, Ethelinda importantly presses on the ways that bibliographical studies, especially those connected to genre, must reckon with how data capturing reinforces binaries and thereby is unequipped to make space for sexuality or for fluid gender identities.

Ethelinda Margaretta Potts (née Thorpe) came from a prominent family, was financially stable, and had every social privilege to support her life as a wife and mother. These general details, however, do not account for her personal life, identity, and literary legacy. Though she published multiple works, some in more than one edition, Ethelinda does not appear in the *Orlando Database of Women Writers* and is mentioned only briefly in J.R. de J. Jackson's *Bibliography of Romantic Poetry*.[63] She is, as were many women writers who published anonymously during this period, elusive. Ethelinda Margaretta was born in Bexley, Kent, in 1758, the daughter of prominent local antiquarian John Thorpe, Esq. (1715–1792), and his wife, Catherina Holker (1728–1789). Thorpe studied medicine and was the son of Dr. John Thorpe (1682–1750), a physician and Fellow of the Royal Society. Catherina Holker was also the child of a physician, Dr. Lawrence Holker (1692–1738). Catherina was to inherit Bourne Place, a large manor house and surrounding lands in Bexley, from her brother on his death, but since she predeceased him, her daughters, Catherina and Ethelinda, became his coheirs.[64] Ethelinda's elder sister, Catherina (1750–1821), married Thomas Meggison (1750–1822), a solicitor from Kent in 1779. Together the Thorpe daughters had a robust and respected extended family in the area.

In 1784, Ethelinda Thorpe married Cuthbert Potts (1743–1825), a surgeon. For Cuthbert, Ethelinda was a good match—her family was connected in the medical profession, and she came with property and income.[65] Ethelinda's father and her father-in-law, also named Cuthbert Potts (1699–1769), were both original contributors to *The Gentlemen's Magazine* and wrote for other publications in their areas of interest (antiquarianism and medicine, respectively).[66] Ethelinda therefore came from an intellectual and literary-minded family, so it is not surprising that she would publish her own writings later on. Together, she and Cuthbert had three surviving children: Lawrence Holker Potts (1789), Cuthberta Ethelinda Potts (1790), and Michael Le'Flemming Potts (1791). It appears, however, that following the birth of their youngest son (or possibly before), the Pottses' marriage ruptured.

On Thursday, June 9, 1796, an advertisement ran on the first page of *The Sun* under the heading "Fifty Pounds Reward" stating that "Ethelinda Margaretta Potts, the Wife of Cuthbert Potts, of Pall-Mall, in the Parish of St. James, Westminister [*sic*], Surgeon, has absented herself from her said Husband, and cruelly abandoned her Three Infant Children." This advertisement, laying bare the Pottses' marital discord, aimed "to give Notice . . . that whoever inform her said Husband, where the aforesaid Ethelinda Margaretta Potts now secrets herself, so that she may be secured, shall receive a Reward of Fifty Pounds." The advertisement calls Ethelinda an "ungrateful Woman and unnatural Mother." Potts also attached an unflattering physical description of his wife to aid in her discovery and hints at her mental illness or instability by what he calls "the corroding canker on her mind." The advertisement seeking to secure the return of his wife certainly takes no steps to safeguard her reputation. Potts's advertisement reveals further information about Ethelinda by providing the physical description of Langford, "her companion, who attends her." Langford, the ad reads, "rarely appears by day" and "is supposed to have several places of residence, in and out of Town, some of which are probably not far distant from the office of the City Solicitor, Guildhall, London."[67] These taken together suggest that Langford is either a sex worker or is involved in other nefarious and illegal operations. This "Fifty Pound Reward" advertisement ran again in *The Sun* on Saturday, June 11, and was reprinted as a handbill (Figure 4.2) to be distributed, presumably, to the wider London public.[68]

Cuthbert Potts's reasons for wanting his wife's return may sit outside the mere desire to reunite with his spouse and bring home the mother of his children. A Chancery lawsuit, *Meggison versus Moore*, had been decided the previous year. It had been brought by Thomas Meggison and his wife, Catherina Thorpe Meggison (Ethelinda's sister), their heirs, and the Pottses, who argued that they were equal heirs of the late Lawrence Holker, Esq., their uncle, and was based on Holker making several codicils to his will.[69] This case and its exact wording explain Cuthbert Potts's willingness to make public his wife's abandonment of him. His interest in this case is financial—specifically, what income from his estranged wife's inheritance he could expect as her husband. The judge listed "Mr. and Mrs. Potts" together as "entitled to equal monies" divided with Catherina and Thomas Meggison. Potts may have hoped to use this language to argue for his right to Ethelinda's fortune, since by law, all of a woman's possessions and property reverted to her husband upon marriage. Ethelinda's uncle, however, had taken care to provide for her financial independence by granting her an annuity "for her natural life *for her sole and separate use*" (emphasis mine). With the support of this annuity, and perhaps her entire inheritance, Ethelinda was able to flee her marriage, which we can only assume was no longer amenable to her. We do not know the outcome of Potts's attempt to find Ethelinda or whether he gained control over her finances. But in the advertisement, Potts paints Ethelinda as a selfish, negligent wife and an unfit mother—great crimes for an eighteenth-century woman.

Ethelinda's collection of verses might not be a novel as we know or understand the genre, and it certainly confused contemporary critics, but having learned from the case of Fanshawe the rich and worthy literary histories that may lie outside the strict scope we have defined for our data, I pursued Ethelinda's story to better understand what *Moonshine* was and what we might learn from it. A reading of the publication history of *Moonshine* and some of the poetry therein tells a different story of Ethelinda, her "companion" Langford, and her children and grandchildren than the one Cuthbert Potts publishes—one of love, longing, and how middling women still managed to build a life when

Fifty Pounds Reward!

WHEREAS, ETHELINDA MARGARETTA POTTS, the Wife of CUTHBERT POTTS, of Pall-Mall, in the Parish of St. James, Westminster, Surgeon, hath absented herself from her said Husband, and cruelly abandoned her Three Infant Children:

And whereas, a certain young Attorney has boasted, that he will protect this ungrateful Woman and unnatural Mother, affecting a disregard of Consequences which may arise from a CORRESPONDENCE, now in the Press, with also a Sketch of the eventful History of this great little Man, whose Mind, as well as Form, seems stamp'd and impress'd from the same Mint; also displaying the Finesse, Tricks, and Manœuvres of his Colleagues, and of his many Predecessors in the honourable Office of this Lady's Attorney.

This is to give Notice, notwithstanding the Vaunting of this virtuous Limb of the Law, that whoever will inform her said Husband, where the aforesaid ETHELINDA MARGARETTA POTTS now secrets herself, so that she may be secured, shall receive a Reward of FIFTY POUNDS, by applying as above.

N. B. In her person she is short and corpulent, her Face round and bloated, a pale Complexion, and a full dark blue Eye, a Nose rather aquiline, and in the lower part of her Face she has a strong family Likeness to her only Sister, the worthy Lady of Thomas Meggison, of Hatton-Garden, Solicitor, and of Whalton, near Morpeth, in Northumberland, Esq. She is about the age of Forty, though the corroding Canker on her Mind marks an older look; her Speech, which is generally introduced with a hem! is slow and distinct; her Voice low, without cadence, with a singular Monotony.

Her Companion, who attends her, is SALLY LANGFORD, in Stature also low, and in Person uninteresting;—a flat Face, with a turn-up or pug Nose, a quick and animated Eye, and is well known at the Fives-Court, St. Martin's-Street, Leicester-square, where her Father is a Stringer of Racquets.

This Lady rarely appears by day; she has been seen frequently at a notable Toy-shop, in Fleet-Street, facing the new Clock of St. Dunstan's Church. She is supposed to have several Places of Residence, in and out of Town, some of which are probably not far distant from the Office of the City Solicitor, Guildhall, London.

The Sun, June 9, 1796,

Figure 4.2. Reward handbill published by Cuthbert Potts, reprinted from *The Sun*, June 9, 1796. Bodleian Libraries, University of Oxford, N11748461. 1 sheet; 1/4to.

their reputation was crushed. *Moonshine* reminds us that creative and imaginative writing are, for many marginalized peoples, the only way they could (legally and possibly) record their lives.

Twenty-five years after Ethelinda purportedly abandoned her husband and children, her two-volume *Moonshine* (1814) was printed in London. Her dedication reads: "Dear Children, To augment your fondness for your brother, to you, behold him sent, by me, your loving MOTHER." She goes on to address "the stranger" reader, explaining that she has published the work so that her friends might more easily access her writings.[70] This address's insistence on an intimate audience for the books falls much in line with other prefatory traditions outlined in Chapter 2, as does her exclamation in the poetical "Preface" that she hopes her book will by its unimportance be "'scaping [the] critics" notice. A later poem in the prefatory section entitled "The Manuscript Just Bound" expresses her anxiety at meeting with book reviewers: "The mere idea of printing, so filled my head with thoughts of the public and critics, that those august bodies are frequently mentioned in my reveries."[71]

Perhaps these prefatory posturings are what caused the *Critical* to place *Moonshine* among the ranks of "Novels." Ethelinda's anxieties show that she thought of herself as a writer who made herself vulnerable to attacks by critics once in print rather than as only a part-time scribbler of private verses. If the *Critical*'s reviewer read only these prefatory pages before penning their aricle, it may be *Moonshine*'s alignment with other novel prefatory traditions that caused this critic to classify the work as a novel. This is an explanation we could not have known without examining reviewing as a literary system. It also suggests that a study of the possible preface and review dialogue for poetry during this period might be informative in the case of *Moonshine*, other poetical works, and their authors.

Amid the poems referencing critics, novel writing, reading, and authorship, there are also many poems in the collection that expound on a long and loving relationship between Ethelinda and her children. These poems show maternal love in both memories and reflections. There are sweet occasional poems, like "On My Daughter Bringing Flowers to my Pillow" and "On my Son—, at—."[72] In "On my Son Sending Me The Flower of a Midnight Ceres, in His Winter Gloves," the writer recalls of the gift: "A challenge far from scorn'd, this glove / Is hoarded by maternal love" (ln. 9–10).[73]

A pensive piece, "My Children," calls up the ghosts of memories in "a little room, / that's low and narrow as a tomb" and the scraps of conversation and events that happened there (ln. 1–2). Jumping forward in time, Ethelinda notes that when her grown children, "young men come down, / to tell me all about the Town," their visit does not include discussion about their penknives or the tedium of putting on coats, as it did when they were small, but about what they read of in the news (ln. 15–16). In the poem, Ethelinda reaches out with hope, conjuring an image of her children in the future: "I see that day when on each other, / You look, and recollect, / YOUR MOTHER" (ln. 27–29). A footnote to this poem dates it to after Potts's public campaign against her but acknowledges those as difficult years: "Several pieces concerning my children, previous to the year 1801, are not inserted; being of too pensive and peculiar a turn."[74] Because all evidence points to Ethelinda being financially solvent, it is unlikely that she published these poems in attempt to make a profit, and in fact she may have footed the cost of publication herself.[75] The dedication to her children suggests a hope of reinforcing her affection for her two youngest, who would have experienced their most formative years amid their parents' marital strife.

Following *Moonshine*'s first appearance in 1814, Ethelinda continued to publish a series of works with that title. Bibliographically we would define these books as completely new texts rather than new editions of the first work, but for her, they seem to continue the personal ruminations of the poetry in her 1814 volume. The title page of her 1832 *Moonshine* proclaims it to be a second edition of her 1814 work. These two 1832 volumes, however, subtitled "containing sketches in England and Whales" and "containing Miscellaneous Trifles," respectively, contain only a few poems from the 1814 *Moonshine* and are otherwise newly published poems focused on travel. The 1832 *Moonshine* is dedicated "to my children and grandchildren" and features a small paragraph declaring that "The following pages were composed in the *night*" and "can be no acquisition to the stranger."[76]

An 1833 edition of the same title with more poetry and some added plates is issued with the 1832 subtitles but still claims on its title pages to be the second edition, and in 1835, a third volume is issued—presumably to be added to the 1833 edition, with the subtitle "containing unconnected trifles and appendix."[77] This 1835 volume reprints several poems from the 1814 *Moonshine* and includes a smattering of other odd items: excerpts of letters from illustrious people to whom Ethelinda sent copies of her poetry or who saw her "shell-work"—a common art form of intricately arranged seashells into images—on display at St. James Palace, excerpts from her father's publications, poems written by family members, and a family history of the Thorpes and Holkers in the form of a letter addressed to "My Dear Grandchildren." It also includes a poem dated April 1835, almost a year exactly before her death, entitled "Before Day-Break, The Preceding Evening Was Thus Described To Give A Moment's Relief from Legal and Other Cares."[78] Perhaps Ethelinda was making a will, or perhaps legal issues relating to her inheritance or her estrangement from her husband dogged her until her death. Poems such as "To each of my grandchildren on receiving letters from them," "Lines from my son," "Verses inscribed to the most affectionate of mothers, by her daughter, CEP [Cuthberta Ethelinda Potts], when fifteen years of age," and "Lines by CEP" all suggest that Ethelinda had regular and loving contact with her children and grandchildren.[79]

The maternal poems in these collections encourage us to read against Cuthbert Potts's insistence that Ethelinda was an "unnatural" mother and to be ever mindful of the heavy hand that men have in the official documents of history. While *Moonshine* is not generically what we now understand as a novel, the *Critical*'s placement of it in that section of its Monthly Catalogue perhaps pushed it into the view of a different readership than it intended, as it has for this monograph. Ethelinda Margaretta Potts and her *Moonshine* have never been the subject of scholarly attention, and the prevalence of Cuthbert Potts's published version of events could otherwise have stood as Ethelinda's history had not I explored this item.

Ethelinda's estrangement from her husband is also the story of a queer woman carving out her own life in the Romantic period. Abandoning her heterosexual marriage for her Sapphic "companion" Langford—so named in Potts's advertisement—Ethelinda represents a writer who, because she lives outside of the eighteenth-century expectations of a woman married to a man, with several children, also falls outside our field of vision when we define and look for authorial identity.[80] Ethelinda's life and works highlight how understanding gender as a contributor to genre is incomplete without considering sexuality as well. As Susan Lanser illustrates, "sexuality *is* history" and plays an integral role in the making of literary history. Sexuality presses upon history to carve out the very forms and events that define it.[81] Slandering her as a runaway mother and naming the accomplice of her estrangement, Potts suggests that he and his children were angry and hurt by Ethelinda's moving away from them. But the poetry about and from her children in *Moonshine* suggest that Ethelinda enjoyed a loving relationship with them even after she left her husband. Further investigation into Ethelinda's poetry and the lives of her children also shows Langford in a congenial relationship with Ethelinda's family.

Like many English family trees, those of the Pottses and Thorpes show they were prolific in their use of legacy names. In each successive generation, we see children bearing the names of family members or those with important connections to the family. Ethelinda's daughter Cuthberta Ethelinda, for example, wears a familial name combining that of her parents. Ethelinda's oldest son, Laurence Holker Potts, was named for his great uncle and great grandfather, and he in turn continued this tradition of naming his children for members of his family. Laurence Holker Potts's children—Ethelinda, Cuthberta, Laurence

Holker Jr., John Thorpe, and Catherina Thorpe—all feature family names, mostly for his maternal family. These names do not suggest an estrangement from his mother. Laurence's second child, a daughter who lived only ten months, was christened Ann Sarah Langford Potts in 1822.[82] It appears that Ethelinda met this short-lived grandchild; her poem "On Miss——, Being Awakened By Candlelight" (I, 89) declares that "Ann smiles when other babes would weep" (ln. 1).[83] Though this daughter bearing the name of Ethelinda's companion died young, Laurence Holker Potts went on to name his youngest child in her stead as well: Benjamin Langford Forster Potts (1839–1910).[84] Clearly Langford was not viewed by the Potts children as a villain; in naming his children for her, Laurence Potts identifies her as family.

Langford also features repeatedly in Ethelinda's poetry. References to Sarah or Miss L—d are scattered across *Moonshine's* editions and fold back on one another in their footnotes and contextual references. Because Ethelinda does not publish her poems chronologically, the relationship between them is collapsed in a series of cross-references. This may be an intentional obscuring of her relationship with Langford, or it may simply be that though one's everyday life is most revealing to us as modern historians, for those living it, it is unremarkable. If, as Ethelinda's prefaces often repeat, these were truly published for the pleasure and use of her friends, there would be no need to hide the presence of Langford in occasional poems about her life or to explain her presence in them.

Appearing first in the 1832 edition of *Moonshine* in a poem called "the Dream," Sarah is one of two women riding in a boat on a Welsh river.[85] In her 1835 "To Sir Henry Halford, Bart."—a well-known physician—Ethelinda exclaims at her own recovery from illness and declares in gratitude that "Kind heaven vouchsafed our hopes to bless, / And I my Sarah still possess" (ln. 3–4).[86] She evidently worried over the illness taking her from *her* Sarah. A footnote to this poem identifies the Sarah as "Miss L—d" and sends the reader to the aforesaid dream poem to connect the two figures. The dream poem and others in the collection are very specific in their geography and seem to be inspired by Ethelinda's Welsh travels (for which a full itinerary is included in the 1835 volume three) and her visit to Llangollen—made famous by Eleanor Butler and Sarah Ponsonby, a queer couple known as the Ladies of Llangollen and renowned for moving to Wales to live together outside of heterosocial norms. Sarah likely accompanied Ethelinda on this journey, as evidenced by "the Dream" and all Ethelinda's travel notes in the text.

Sarah shows up in more intimate poetical scenes as well. A section written at Sidmouth Beach near Exeter dated July 20, 1822, records a ship, ironically named the *Sally*, wrecking there while Ethelinda was staying nearby. She was "awakened by something . . . and went to Miss L—, who striking a light, we could not find anything to prevent my again going to rest."[87] Miss L— is sleeping nearby and attempting to comfort Ethelinda when she is startled in the night. A poem sequence in the 1835 volume "On my Dear Friend" records their long connection and appears to contain poems from across their acquaintance. It begins with an occasional "Written on the Present of a Screen" remembrance: "The night when first my friend I saw, / near twice twelve years has not effaced / . . . In memory of that night, you guess, / For then the stars to me were kind" (ln. 1–2; 7–8). A later poem in this sequence states: "With thee I have mountains cross'd," providing further evidence that the women traveled together (ln. 1).

Of their friendship, the poet declares: "By more than thrice twelve queens of May; / with only thee have dragg'd whole years / . . . of thee friend, I never tire . . . But twixt our hearts love has so long / Remain'd through time their unions strong" (ln. 4–5; 8; 12–13).[88] The last lines in this sequence declare: "These [children] by descent possess my love, / But you to me are treasure trove; / And should we look this world around, / How few have such a treasure found" (ln. 1–4). These closing sentiments show that Ethelinda values the bond she has with her children and grandchildren, who "by descent" have a right to her affection, but also does not fail to "treasure" the woman who spent 36 years as her intimate. These devoted lines, only published in the volume that appeared the year before her death, show us a tenderness that Ethelinda did not reveal in her earlier editions.

Ethelinda and Langford sit at an intersectional queerness—their relationship also includes issues of class, as Ethelinda is an heiress from a wealthy family and Langford is, as far as I can tell, of a more working-class status. Ethelinda's identity may also touch on ability, as she frequently writes about her health. These identities are evident as well in the description that Ethelinda's husband publishes, which pushes the concept of the lesbian "monster"—mentally unsound and socially and morally reprehensible for straying from the heteronormative expectations of her compulsory marriage to a man and the bearing of his children. When Bonnie Ruberg, Jason Boyd, and James Howe ask in "Toward a Queer Digital Humanities" where queerness exists or thrives in Digital Humanities (DH) work, they importantly argue in answer that "queerness can function as a force to destabilize and restructure the way that DH scholarship is done."[89]

As the *NRD* is a work of intersectional feminism, I had intended it to do just this, but as this chapter shows, the results of such work are often unexpected. Ruber, Boyd, and Howe echo Klein and Ezell's insistence that we attune to women in our data and to the pieces that do not fit when they argue that "moving toward a queer digital humanities means valuing queer lives and embracing a queer ethos but also addressing actionable, concrete ways that queerness can shift how the work of DH is done."[90] The *NRD* does not and cannot track sexuality. The practice of assigning a gender to the writers captured in the *NRD* also makes an argument about binary gender, one that cannot illustrate the various ways these writers might have identified personally or presented themselves in their authorial personas. These are shortcomings that I acknowledge and hope *NRD* users will keep in their minds when referring to this data where gender and sexuality are concerned.

Generically, *Moonshine* shows Ethelinda engaged with poetical traditions of the late eighteenth and early nineteenth centuries. The subjects of her verses range from sleep, friendship, flowers, and gardens to classical and modern texts and authors. Many of the poems jostle for page space with extensive footnotes, similar to Smith's *Beachy Head*, highlighting the expanse of the author's intellectual knowledge and personal associations with peoples and places mentioned. A section entitled "Tales" is similar in style to Frances James Child's collection of Northern Ballads and those of Thomas Percy and Robert Burns. Later volumes are chiefly about travel in Bath, Hereford, and Wales, and volume two includes a second preface-like message to the reader that notes "the only apology to be made for saving these Sketches and notes from the flames, would be the possibility of their being of some little use to the female invalid" who cannot travel.[91] This section reads partly like a travel guide, even including a table of "the distances that we were charged" around the area that outlines her own travel itinerary.[92] These pages reveal a writer who resists mainstream society in many forms: She maintains independent control of her inheritance even while married, refuses to stay in a marriage where she is unhappy, does not consider her estrangement from her husband to translate to an estrangement from her children, and builds a life of literary pursuits and travel with Langford.

Ethelinda's publication practices also eschew the ways we understand editions and even (it seems) elude the genre parameters of eighteenth-century critics. She is exactly the kind of writer whom selection practices predicated on heteronormative authorial identifiers, genre markers, and more leave out. I am not surprised that when we apply Klein, and Ezell's insistence that we attend to women in our data wherever we see them and embrace what we find there, Ethelinda's story comes into focus. Because "queer DH scholarship must [itself] be multivalent, multiplicative, and self-critical: a set of practices in flux," I hope that this chapter makes clear that questioning our own work and struggles with our data/subjects should be at the heart of our scholarship and should be explored by future users of the *NRD*.[93] Though Ethelinda's work stands out from the other texts in this cohort because it is largely made up of autobiographical poems rather than prose, an examination of its publication history and authorship shows us how the works of writers resisting social norms may also resist literary parameters. Should we endeavor to write a literary history that rectifies the marginalization of these voices in history, we scholars must also broaden, reexamine, and hold space for the unexpected ways that such literatures may be presented to us.

I hope that my transparency in these case studies helps provide detailed citations of primary sources for use by future scholars. I also hope that they will serve as secondary-scholarship resources for entering these writers into our base-knowledge systems like dictionaries and encyclopedias. Exploring how these authors are treated in their contemporary literary systems and how those systems still perpetuate and influence our genre- and value-related arguments today is central to the work of recovery, and as Kirstyn Leuner argues, "recovery requires identifying the writer's corporeal identity in relation to her corpus." This is essential on many levels because "women's writing is evidence not only of their physical and intellectual writing and labor but also of their bodily existence."[94] The existence of writers of intersectional identities is regularly obscured. Scholars therefore must be willing to probe not only the avenues we set out to investigate in our studies but also those that inherently resist our studies. We cannot fail to acknowledge that when we study gender through quantitative means, that work is, as Laura Mandell argues, "a means of counting people counting."[95] The obscuring of these individuals is not an accident of data but a purposeful statement of their "not counting" on the larger stage of literary history and is therefore not feminist research at all. Our resistant data are evidence of a richer history of the English novel, one that the *NRD* has helped us here only to glimpse.

Postscript

———————————————————

As is so often the case with narratives based on recovery, we don't know what we don't know until someone finds the example that forces a reexamination of categories and criteria.[1]

When I began to conduct research on book review periodicals, I thought that I would be writing about marketing and bibliographical elements like type size and page space. I expected to find more to say about the arrangement of the physical book than the rhetorical movements therein. And while some of the arguments in this book do derive from material evidences like those listed, I found the voices and experiences of women in book history in a way that I had not anticipated. Women were present in a place where I had been taught to expect them to be absent.

In response to the 2018 Women's Book History symposium (of which I was a participant), Margaret Ezell argues that "one of the steps that was essential to the recovery of physical evidence [of women's book history] was recognizing the extent to which the conditions creating their invisibility came from the narratives we had inherited about women who wrote, why they wrote, and what the social consequences for women's writing were."[2] I expected the Reviews to lead me to a largely male-dominated venue, where what my research would have to offer would *only* be what the Reviews argued *about* women—the inherited narrative. I had no idea that I would find the women themselves in the dialogues their prefaces enter into, in Charlotte Smith's continued labor, in Althea Fanshawe's diary, and in Ethelinda Potts's paratext. I am grateful that I believed in the Reviews as a site of women's writing even before I had such extensive proof, which pushed my "reexamination of categories and criteria" scholars had heretofore used to study Reviews and women writers.[3]

Looking forward to the future of women's book history and what scholars today have learned from one another, Margaret Ezell, Betty Schellenberg, and Michelle Levy make two important points that I have leaned heavily on: There is a need for a multiplicity of narratives of history if we hope to include women and other marginalized people in them and for an attunement to the extensive labor that this recovery work requires.[4] I write candidly on the latter so that there can be no doubt among other scholars that projects such as this one require a great commitment of time and labor now to attempt to uncover the works and labor of women past. I fear that if I do not make women's book history and recovery work transparent, I will be complicit in "making women's literary work from the past visible and sustainable" at the "risk of enabling [feminist scholars'] own invisibility within the discipline and in the academy."[5]

To write women's book history into the field of book history itself and into literary history and the canon, we must look to the examples of earlier recovery work that help us imagine what we do not know and seek what we have been told is not there in history for us to find. This project has been an undertaking ten-plus years in the making, and it will undoubtedly have flaws. Even while we work to fill the silences in the conspicuously genderless histories we have inherited, new ones will emerge. It should not be our endeavor to fill *all* such lapses—this is impossible to ask of historical documents that were not written or preserved for the methods we now put them to. Rather, we must attune our scholarship to an awareness of these gaps, so that even in their absences, they are present in our methodologies and conclusions.

Contents of *Anna Laetitia Barbauld's* The British Novelists *and Sir Walter Scott's* Ballantyne's British Novelists

The British Novelists
Edited by Anna Laetitia Barbauld (1810)

Vols.	Author	Title	Original Date of Publication
1–8	Samuel Richardson	*Clarissa*	1748
9–15	Samuel Richardson	*Sir Charles Grandison*	1753
16–17	Daniel Defoe	*Robinson Crusoe*	1719
18	Henry Fielding	*Joseph Andrews*	1742
18–21	Henry Fielding	*Tom Jones*	1749
22	Clara Reeve	*The Old English Baron*	1777
22	Horace Walpole	*The Castle of Otranto*	1764
23	Samuel Coventry	*Pompey the Little*	1751
23	Oliver Goldsmith	*The Vicar of Wakefield*	1766
24–25	Charlotte Lennox	*The Female Quixote*	1752
26	Samuel Johnson	*Rasselas*	1759
26	John Hawkesworth	*Almoran and Hamet*	1761
27	Frances Brooke	*Lady Julia Mandeville*	1763
27	Elizabeth Inchbald	*Nature and Art*	1796
28	Elizabeth Inchbald	*A Simple Story*	1791
29	Henry Mackenzie	*The Man of Feeling*	1771
29	Henry Mackenzie	*Julia de Roubigne, A Tale*	1777
30–31	Tobias Smollett	*Humphry Clinker*	1771
32–33	Richard Graves	*The Spiritual Quixote*	1773
34–35	John Moore	*Zeluco*	1789
36–37	Charlotte Smith	*The Old Manor House*	1793
38–39	Frances Burney	*Evelina*	1778
40–42	Frances Burney	*Cecilia*	1782
43–44	Ann Radcliffe	*The Romance of the Forest*	1791
45–47	Ann Radcliffe	*The Mysteries of Udolpho*	1794
48	Robert Bage	*Hermsprong*	1796
49–50	Maria Edgeworth	*Belinda*	1801
50	Maria Edgeworth	*The Modern Griselda*	1805

Ballantyne's British Novelists
Edited by Sir Walter Scott (1821–1824)

Vols.	Author	Title	Original Date of Publication
1	Henry Fielding	*Joseph Andrews*	1742
(1821)	Henry Fielding	*Tom Jones*	1749
	Henry Fielding	*Amelia*	1751
	Henry Fielding	*Jonathan Wilde*	1743
2	Tobias Smollett	*Roderick Random*	1748
(1821)	Tobias Smollett	*Peregrine Pickle*	1751
	Tobias Smollett	*Humphry Clinker*	1771
3	Tobias Smollett	*Count Fathom*	1753
(1821)	Tobias Smollett	*Sir Launcelot Greaves*	1760
	Tobias Smollett	Cerventes' *Don Quixote*	1755
4	Tobias Smollett	*Gil Blas*	1748
(1822)	Alain Le Sage	*The Devil on Two Sticks*	1707
	Alain Le Sage	*Vanillo Gonzales*	1734
	Charles Johnstone	*The Adventures of a Guinea*	1760
5	Laurence Sterne	*Tristram Shandy*	1759
(1823)	Laurence Sterne	*Sentimental Journey*	1768
	Oliver Goldsmith	*The Vicar of Wakefield*	1766
	Samuel Johnson	*Rasselas*	1759
	Henry Mackenzie	*The Man of Feeling*	1771
	Henry Mackenzie	*The Man of the World*	1773
	Henry Mackenzie	*Julia de Roubigne*	1777
	Horace Walpole	*The Castle of Otranto*	1764
	Clara Reeve	*The Old English Baron*	1777
6–8	Samuel Richardson	*Pamela*	1740
(1824)	Samuel Richardson	*Clarissa*	1748
	Samuel Richardson	*Sir Charles Grandison*	1753
9	Jonathan Swift	*Gulliver's Travels*	1726
(1824)	Robert Bage	*Mount Henneth*	1782
	Robert Bage	*Barham Downs*	1784
	Robert Bage	*James Wallace*	1788
	Richard Cumberland	*Henry*	1795
10	Ann Radcliffe	*Sicilian Romance*	1790
(1824)	Ann Radcliffe	*Romance of the Forest*	1791
	Ann Radcliffe	*The Mysteries of Udolpho*	1794
	Ann Radcliffe	*The Italian*	1797
	Ann Radcliffe	*Castles of Athlin and Dunbayne*	1789

55 Novels in the NRD *that are not in Garside, Raven, and Schöwerling's* Bibliography of Prose Fiction, 1770–1829

	NRD Catalog #	Title	English Author/ Translator
1	1789.72	The Adventures of Theagenes and Chariclea. A Romance	Anon.
2	1790.75	Norman Tales	Anon.
3	1790.76	The Effects of Vanity; or, Mary Meanwell and Kitty Pertly, a Tale written for the Use of the Sunday Schools	Anon.
4	1793.46	Mental Improvement for a Young Lady, on her Entrance into the World, addressed to a favourite Niece	Green, Sarah
5	1794.57	Selico, an African Tale, translated into English Verse, from the French Prose of M. de Florian	Anon.
6	1794.58	Amusement Hall; or, an Easy Introduction to the Attainment of useful Knowledge	Neale, Hannah [from English Short Title Catalogue of the 2nd ed.]
7	1794.59	The Life and Extraordinary Adventures of James Molesworth Hobart, alias Henry Griffin, alias Lord Massey, the New-Market Duke of Ormond, &c. involving a number of well-known Characters: together with a short Sketch of the early part of the Life of Dr. Torquid	Collard, John
8	1795.51	Ivan Czarowitz, or the Rose without Prickles that stings not. A Tale	Anon.
9	1795.52	The Comforts of Arabella, the Daughter of Amanda	Anon.
10	1796.92	Ariel; or, a Picture of the Human Heart	Dutton, Thomas
11	1796.93	Tales of the Minstrels	Anon.
12	1796.94	Henrietta, Princess Royal of England. An Historical Novel	Anon.
13	1798.76	Easter Holidays; or, Domestic Conversations, designed for the Instruction, and, it is hoped, for the Amusement of Young People	Fanshawe, Althea

	NRD Catalog #	Title	English Author/ Translator
14	1799.00	Marmontel's Tales, Selected and abridged, for the Instruction and Amusement of Youth	Pilkington, Mary
15	1800.82	Arabian Nights Entertainments, &c.	Anon.
16	1800.83	The Story of Al-Raoui, a Tale from the Arabic	Anon. [Possibly William Beckford, or his "copyist" Anne-Marie Fauques de Vaucluse]
17	1800.84	Edward, a Tale; for young Persons. Principally founded upon that much-admired Performance of the same Name, by Dr. Moore; and adopted for the Capacities of Youth	Pilkington, Mary
18	1801.73	The Moral Legacy; or, Simple Narratives	Anon.
19	1801.74	The Little Mountaineers of Auvergne; or, the Adventures of James and Georgette	Anon.
20	1801.75	Eight Historical Tales, curious and instructive	Unknown [preface is signed "J. W."; under printers imprint on title page is printed "By H. Bryer, Bridewell Hospital, Bridge Street"]
21	1801.76	The Sincere Huron; or Pupil of Nature: a true History	Ashmore, Francis
22	1802.62	A Series of Novels	Anon.
23	1802.63	The Travels of Alladin, Sultan of Egypt. An Eastern allegorical Story	Anon.
24	1803.80	Lucy Osmond. A Story	LeFanu, Elizabeth
25	1803.81	Daphnis and Chloe, a pastoral Novel, now first secretly translated into English from the original Greek of Longus	Anon. Translator: Charles Valentine Le Grice [a la Princeton catalogue copy]
26	1804.74	Letters from Mrs. Palmerstone to her Daughter	Hunter, Rachel
27	1804.75	Harry Clinton. A Tale for Youth	Hays, Mary
28	1805.76	The Twin Sisters; or, the Advantages of Religion	Sandham, Elizabeth
29	1805.77	Memoirs of a Picture, containing the Adventures of many conspicuous Characters, connected with the Arts, and including a genuine Biographical Sketch of the late Mr. George Morland	Collins, William

	NRD Catalog #	Title	English Author/ Translator
30	1805.78	Love and Satire: containing the Correspondence of Julius and Eliza; to which is prefixed, a few brief Memoirs of an unfortunate Lover	Anon.
31	1805.79	Alfred and Galba: or the History of two Brothers, supposed to be written by themselves. For the Use of young People	Campbell, John
32	1807.70	Memoirs of Sylvester Daggerwood	Pangloss, Peter [pseudonym]
33	1807.71	Tales from Shakespeare, designed for the Use of young Persons	Lamb, Charles
34	1807.72	The Calendar; or Monthly Recreations	Pilkington, Mary
35	1807.73	Bath Characters; or Sketches from Life	Pallet, Peter
36	1808.112	Theodore and Blanche; or the Victims of Love	Anon.
37	1809.80	The Letters of a Peruvian Princess	Mudford, William
38	1809.81	The Travels of Humanius in search of the Temple of Happiness, an Allegory	Lucas, William
39	1811.81	Moral Tales	Cooper, Maria Susanna
40	1811.82	Felissa; or the Life and Opinions of a Kitten of Sentiment; with twelve coloured Engravings	Lamb, Charles
41	1812.67	Rose and Emily, or Sketches of Youth	Roberts, Margaret
42	1813.64	The Wife; or Caroline Herbert	Cooper, Maria Susanna
43	1814.62	The Good Aunt: including the Story of Signor Aldersonini and his Son	Ventum, Harriet
44	1815.55	Popular Models, and Impressive Warnings for the Sons and Daughters of Industry	Grant, Beatrice
45	1815.56	Moonshine. Novel	Potts, Ethelinda Margaretta Thorpe
46	1815.57	The History of Little Davy's New Hat	Bloomfield, Robert
47	1815.58	The Brothers, or Consequences	Hays, Mary
48	1815.59	Ellen the Teacher; a Tale for Youth	Hofland, Barbara [née Hoole]
49	1815.60	Paternal Love; or, The Reward of Friendship	Darling, Peter Middleton
50	1816.60	The Life and Adventures of Peter Wilkins, a Cornish-Man: taken from his own Mouth, in his Passage to England, from off Cape Horn in America, in the Ship Hector	Paltock, Robert
51	1817.56	The Tale of Edward and Anna, a Fragment	Anon.
52	1817.57	Family Annals, or The Sisters	Hays, Mary

	NRD Catalog #	Title	English Author/ Translator
53	1817.58	The Cavern of Roseville; or, The Two Sisters. A Tale	Jamieson, Alexander
54	1817.59	Rosa; or, Village Incidents	Anon.
55	1820.71	The Young Countess, a Tale for Youth	Pinchard, Elizabeth

Introduction

1. Frances Burney, *Evelina: Or the History of A Young Lady's Entrance into the World*, ed. Edward A. Bloom (Oxford: Oxford University Press, 2002).

2. Frances Burney (Mm D'Arblay) to Dr. Burney, November 8, 1796, in Frances Burney, *Journals and Letters*, ed. Peter Sabor (London: Penguin UK, 2006), vi.

3. Throughout this book, I, like Derek Roper, use "Review" to refer to the periodicals (specifically the *Monthly* and the *Critical*) and "review" to refer to the individual articles within the periodical. Derek Roper, *Reviewing before the Edinburgh, 1788–1802* (Newark, NJ: University of Delaware Press, 1978).

4. Burney, *Journals and Letters*, vii.

5. Burney, *Journals and Letters*, November 14, 1796, viii.

6. Throughout this book, I refer to the period of study as both the eighteenth century and the Romantic period. While the period from 1790 to 1820 covers what is traditionally understood as the Romantic period, the legacy of book reviews and how they function began in the 1750s.

7. For an extensive history of book reviewing in England, see Antonia Forster, *Index to Book Reviews in England, 1775–1800* (London: British Library, 1997); Antonia Forster, "Book Reviewing," in *The Cambridge History of the Book in Britain, 1695–1830*, vol. 3, The Cambridge History of the Book in Britain (Cambridge: Cambridge University Press, 2009), 631–648.

8. This book and accompanying database consider only the *Monthly Review* and the *Critical Review* for two reasons, the first being labor. As both projects are undertaken only by myself, constraints on time, funding, and bandwidth resources caused me to limit which periodicals to study. The second reason is the period of study: Both of these periodicals stretch across most of the period from 1790 to 1820, and as the first established, they were well circulated and read. The many review periodicals that followed the *Monthly* and the *Critical* were at times short-lived or specifically affiliated with a certain goal or audience (political party, intended for women readers, only ran for five years, etc.). A detailed explanation of these choices can be found in the "Procedure for Compiling and Guide for Using the *Novels Reviewed Database, 1790–1820*" on Bibsite.org: https://bibsite .org/Detail/objects/218.

9. Antonia Forster, "Review Journals and the Reading Public," in *Books and Their Readers in Eighteenth-Century England: New Essays*, ed. Isabel Rivers (New York: Continuum, 2001), 176.

10. Joseph F. Bartolomeo, *A New Species of Criticism: Eighteenth-Century Discourse on the Novel* (Newark, NJ: University of Delaware Press, 1994).

11. Laura Runge, "Churls and Graybeards and Novels Written by a Lady: Gender in Eighteenth-Century Book Reviews," *CW3 Journal (Corvey Women Writers 1796–1834 on the Web)* 1 (Summer 2004). The Corvey Collection Database often incorporates quotes from reviews into their discussion of gendered authorship of novels. Frank Donoghue's *Fame Machine* only briefly remembers women in a final chapter as an afterthought.

12. Laura Mandell, "Gender and Cultural Analytics: Finding or Making Stereotypes?," in *Debates in the Digital Humanities 2019*, ed. Matthew K. Gold and Lauren F. Klein (Minneapolis: University of Minnesota Press, 2019), 16.

13. Rachel Scarborough King, "'[L]et a Girl Read': Periodicals and Women's Literary Canon Formation," in *Women's Periodicals and Print Culture in Britain, 1690–1820s: The Long Eighteenth Century*, ed. Jennie Batchelor and Manushag N. Powell, vol. 1, 5 vols. The Edinburgh History of Women's Periodical Culture in Britain (Edinburgh: Edinburgh University Press, 2018), 221–235; Pam Perkins, "Reviewing Femininity: Gender and Genre in the Late Eighteenth- and Early Nineteenth-Century Periodical Press," in *Women's Periodical Culture in Britain, 1690–1820s*, ed. Jennie Batchelor and Manushag N. Powell, vol. 1, 5 vols. The Edinburgh History of Women's Periodical Culture in Britain (Edinburgh, Scotland: Edinburgh University Press, 2018), 250–262.

14. Michael Gamer, "Assimilating the Novel: Reviews and Collections," in *English and British Fiction 1750–1820*, ed. Peter Garside and Karen O'Brien, vol. 2, The Oxford History of the Novel in English (Oxford University Press, 2015), 539.

15. Peter Garside, James Raven, and Rainer Schöwerling, *The English Novel 1770–1829: A Bibliographical Survey of Prose Fiction Published in the British Isles: Volumes I and II* (Oxford: Oxford University Press, 2000).

16. Garside and Raven's bibliographies show that in 1820, male novelists outstrip their female counterparts in novel authorship. A singular reason for this shift has not yet been nailed down, though the profligacy of Sir Walter Scott's *Waverly* novels may have influenced people viewing the genre as less feminine.

17. Hannah Doherty Hudson, *Romantic Fiction and Literary Excess in the Minerva Press Era*, Cambridge Studies in Romanticism (Cambridge: Cambridge University Press, 2023), 9.

18. Elizabeth Neiman, *Minerva's Gothics: The Politics and Poetics of Romantic Exchange, 1780–1820* (Cardiff: University of Wales Press, 2019), 8.

19. Neiman, *Minerva's Gothics*, 1.

20. Neiman, *Minerva's Gothics*, 26.

21. Hudson, *Romantic Fiction*, 28.

22. George Justice, *The Manufacturers of Literature: Writing and the Literary Marketplace in Eighteenth-Century England* (Newark: University of Delaware Press, 2002), 158.

23. Jennie Batchelor and Manushag N. Powell, "Introduction: Women and the Birth of Periodical Culture," in *Women's Periodicals and Print Culture in Britain, 1690–1820s*, ed. Jennie Batchelor and Manushag N. Powell, vol. 1, 5 vols. The Edinburgh History of Women's Periodical Culture in Britain (Edinburgh: Edinburgh University Press, 2018), 1.

24. Kate Ozment, "Rationale for Feminist Bibliography," *Textual Cultures* 13, no. 1 (April 2020): 167.

25. Jennie Batchelor, *The Lady's Magazine (1770–1830) and the Making of Literary*

History, Edinburgh Critical Studies in Romanticism (Edinburgh: Edinburgh University Press, 2022).

26. Batchelor, *The Lady's Magazine*, 35.

27. Batchelor, *The Lady's Magazine*, 9.

28. A few women wrote for the Reviews as well, though they largely attempted to match their style to the larger trends of the journal and hid behind adopted male pronouns in their articles. For more on this practice, see Megan Peiser, "Reviewing Women: Women Reviewers on Women Novelists," in *Women's Periodicals and Print Culture in Britain, 1690–1820s: The Long Eighteenth Century*, ed. Jennie Batchelor and Manushag N. Powell, vol. 1, 5 vols. The Edinburgh History of Women's Periodical Culture in Britain (Edinburgh: Edinburgh University Press, 2018), 236–249.

29. Katherine Bode, "The Equivalence of 'Close' and 'Distant' Reading; or, Toward a New Object for Data-Rich Literary History," *Modern Language Quarterly* 78, no. 1 (2017): 77–106.

30. Bibliographical Society's journal, *The Library*, begun in 1889 and still in print today.

31. Ian Watt, *The Rise of the Novel: Studies in Defoe, Richardson, and Fielding* (Berkeley: University of California Press, 1957); Nancy Armstrong, *Desire and Domestic Fiction: A Political History of the Novel* (Oxford: Oxford University Press, 1990).

32. Andrew Block, *The English Novel, 1740–1850; a Catalogue Including Prose Romances, Short Stories, and Translations of Foreign Fiction* (London: Dawsons of Pall Mall, 1962).

33. William Harlin McBurney, *A Check List of English Prose Fiction, 1700—1739* (Cambridge: Harvard University Press, 1960); Dorothy Blakey, *The Minerva Press, 1790–1820* (Oxford: Printed for the Bibliographical Society at the Oxford University Press, 1939). See Garside and Raven, volume 1, for an extensive overview of indices and checklists of the English Novel.

34. Marta Kvande, "Restoration Printed Fiction: A Comprehensive, Searchable Database," accessed April 9, 2024, http://www.myweb.ttu.edu/mkvanda/RPFsite/index .xml; Leah Orr, *Novel Ventures: Fiction and Print Culture in England, 1690–1730* (Charlottesville: University of Virginia Press, 2017).

35. Anne Stevens, *British Historical Fiction before Scott* (Basingstoke, UK: Palgrave Macmillan, 2010).

36. William Smith Ward, *Literary Reviews in British Periodicals, 1798–1820; a Bibliography with a Supplementary List of General (Non-Review) Articles on Literary Subjects*, 2 vols. (New York: Garland, 1972); Donald Reiman, ed., *The Romantics Reviewed: Contemporary Reviews of British Romantic Writers.*, 1st ed., 9 vols. (New York: Garland, 1972); Antonia Forster, *Index to Book Reviews in England, 1749–1774* (Carbondale: Southern Illinois University Press, 1990); Forster, *Index to Book Reviews in England, 1775–1800*.

37. Roper, *Reviewing before the Edinburgh, 1788–1802*.

38. Bode, "The Equivalence of 'Close' and 'Distant' Reading," 94.

39. Katherine Bode, *A World of Fiction: Digital Collections and the Future of Literary History*, Digital Humanities (Ann Arbor: University of Michigan Press, Australian National University, 2018), 32.

40. Bode, "The Equivalence of 'Close' and 'Distant' Reading," 91.

41. Bode, *A World of Fiction*, 42.

42. Bode, "The Equivalence of 'Close' and 'Distant' Reading," 98.

43. Catherine D'Ignazio and Lauren F. Klein, *Data Feminism* (Cambridge, MA: MIT Press, 2020), 8.

44. D'Ignazio and Klein, *Data Feminism*, 10.

45. Hudson, *Romantic Fiction*, 23.

46. Ozment, "Rationale for Feminist Bibliography," 152.

47. Jerome J. McGann et al., *The Textual Condition* (Princeton, NJ: Princeton University Press, 1991); Paul Eggert, *The Work and The Reader in Literary Studies* (Cambridge, UK: Cambridge University Press, 2019).

48. Ann R. Hawkins and Stephanie Eckroth, eds., *Romantic Women Writers Reviewed*, 9 vols. (London: Routledge, 2011); Northeastern University Women Writers Project, "Women Writers in Review," accessed April 11, 2024, https://www.wwp.northeastern .edu/review/.

49. Batchelor, *The Lady's Magazine*, 4.

50. Peter Garside, "British Fiction 1800–1829: A Database of Production, Circulation, and Reception," 2004, accessed July 17, 2024, http://www.british-fiction.cf.ac.uk/. Michael Treadwell's family scanned 20 binders of his notes on Restoration and Eighteenth-Century British Book Trade and made them available digitally (through Trent University) after Treadwell's sudden death in 1999. The scanned pages are not searchable. https://www .trentu.ca/english/treadwell/.

51. Ina Ferris, *The Achievement of Literary Authority: Gender, History, and the Waverly Novels* (Ithaca, NY: Cornell University Press, 1991).

52. Stephanie Eckroth, "Celebrity and Anonymity in the Monthly Review's Notices of Nineteenth-Century Novels," in *Women Writers and the Artifacts of Celebrity in the Long Nineteenth Century*, ed. Ann R. Hawkins and Maura Ives (Farnham, UK: Ashgate, 2012), 15; Simon Eliot, "Some Trends in British Book Production, 1800–1919," in *Literature in the Marketplace: Nineteenth-Century British Publishing and Reading Practices*, eds. John O. Jordan and Robert L. Patten (Cambridge: Cambridge University Press, 1995), 19.

53. Kate Harrington, "Perpetuating Difference? Corpus Linguistics and the Gendering of Reported Dialogue," in *Gender and Language Research Methodologies*, ed. Kate Harrington et al. (New York: Palgrave Macmillan, 2008), 96.

Chapter 1 · Reading the Review Periodical in Eighteenth-Century England

1. A version of this chapter appeared in *Papers of the Bibliographical Society of America* 111, no. 4 (2017): 491–511.

2. William St. Clair, *The Reading Nation in the Romantic Period* (Cambridge: Cambridge University Press, 2004).

3. Jan Fergus, *Provincial Readers in Eighteenth-Century England* (Oxford: Oxford University Press, 2006).

4. William Cowper, "William Cowper to Samuel Rose: Wednesday, 13 March 1793," in *Electronic Enlightenment*, ed. Robert McNamee et al. (Oxford: Oxford University Press).

5. Koenraad Claes, "The sources of appropriated content in the Lady's Magazine: some tendencies in vols. I to X (1770–1779)," *The Lady's Magazine (1770–1818): Understanding the Emergence of a Genre* (blog), February 16, 2016, http://blogs.kent.ac.uk/ladys -magazine/2016/02/.

6. "Literature" is used by the Reviews in its broadest sense, meaning all learned works in general, including politics, sermons, poetry, drama, mathematics, philosophy, theology, and "even belles lettres," an article for the *Critical Review* notes in the *Public Advertiser*, December 19, 1755, Issue 6599 np [recto of first leaf].

7. *OED Online*, "annals," accessed July 3, 2025.

8. Jennie Batchelor, *The Lady's Magazine (1770–1830) and the Making of Literary History*, Edinburgh Critical Studies in Romanticism (Edinburgh: Edinburgh University Press, 2022), 85.

9. Eve Bannet also outlines a "discontinuous" style of reading where one dips in and out and moves forward and backward in reading, which likely also was applied to periodical reading across the period at hand. See Eve Tavor Bannet, *Eighteenth-Century Manners of Reading: Print Culture and Popular Instruction in the Anglophone Atlantic World* (Cambridge: Cambridge University Press, 2017), 171.

10. *OED Online*, "account," accessed July 3, 2025.

11. *OED Online*, "annals," accessed July 3, 2025; *OED Online*, "account," accessed July 3, 2025.

12. *A Catalogue of the Books Belonging to the Bristol Library Society; To which are Prefixed the Rules of the Institution, and a List of the Subscribers* (Bristol: J. Rudhall, 1798), 26. Jan Fergus and Ruth Porter's research on the book-buying practices of provincial subscribers to the Reviews is also a valuable quantitative study. They show that while individual subscribers were not swayed in their purchasing by the Review criticism, groups of readers, like book clubs, were. See "Provincial Subscribers to the *Monthly* and *Critical Reviews* and Their Book Purchasing," in *Writers, Books, and Trade: An Eighteenth-Century English Miscellany for William B. Todd*, ed. O. M. Brack Jr. (New York: AMS, 1994), 157–176.

13. Edward Jeffery, *A Catalogue of a Large, Extensive, and Valuable Parcel of Books, in Every Science, and in most Languages; Being the Genuine Library of George Galwey Mills, Esq.* (London: 1800), 3.

14. Manushag Powell, *Performing Authorship in Eighteenth-Century English Periodicals* (Lewisburg, PA: Bucknell University Press, 2012), 10.

15. "The Mysteries of Udolpho, a Romance; interspersed with some Pieces of Poetry," *The Critical Review* 2nd ser., 11 (August 1794): 361.

16. "The Mysteries of Udolpho," 362.

17. "The Mysteries of Udolpho," 363

18. "The Mysteries of Udolpho," 372.

19. "Correspondence: Mysteries of Udolpho," *The Critical Review* 2nd ser., 12 (November 1794): 359–360.

20. "The Castle of Roviego," *The Monthly Review* 2nd ser., 58 (January 1809): 101.

21. "William de Montfort," *The Monthly Review* 2nd ser., 58 (January 1809): 101.

22. "Durval and Adelaide," *The Monthly Review* 2nd ser., 19 (April 1796): 454.

23. Joseph Wimpey, *A letter to the authors of the Monthly review* (London, 1771), 2–4.

24. William Cowper, "William Cowper to Reverend William Unwin: Wednesday, 12 June 1782," in *Electronic Enlightenment*, ed. Robert McNamee et al. (Oxford: Oxford University Press).

25. "Poems," *The Monthly Review* 67 (October 1782): 262–265.

26. Carol Percy, "How Eighteenth-Century Book Reviewers Became Language Guard-

ians," in *Social Roles and Language Practices in Late Modern English*, ed. Päivi Pahta, Minna Nevala, and Arja Nurmi (Amsterdam: Benjamins, 2010), 55–85.

27. George Wilson, "George Wilson to Jeremy Bentham: Thursday, 5 June 1788," in *Electronic Enlightenment*, ed. Robert McNamee et al. (Oxford: Oxford University Press).

28. Hester Lynch Piozzi, "Hester Lynch Piozzi to Reverend Leonard Chappelow: Thursday, 18 June 1801," in *Electronic Enlightenment*, ed. Robert McNamee et al. (Oxford: Oxford University Press).

29. "Retrospection: or a Review of the most striking and important Events, Characters, Situations, and their Consequences, which the last Eighteen Hundred Years have presented to the View of Mankind," *The Critical Review* 2nd ser., 38 (May 1801): 35.

30. H. L. Piozzi, "Letter," *The Gentleman's Magazine: And Historical Chronicle* (July 1801): 602–603.

31. Not including transcriptions of passages exerted from the work under review—see rationale and details on what is included in the *NRD* in "Procedure for Compiling and Guide for Using the *Novels Reviewed Database, 1790–1820*," BibSite, accessed July 3, 2025, https://bibsite.org/Detail/objects/218.

32. See Benjamin Nangle, *The Monthly Review, First Series, 1749–1789: Indexes of Contributors and Articles* (Oxford: Clarendon, 1934); and *The Monthly Review, Second Series, 1790–1815: Indexes of Contributors and Articles* (Oxford: Clarendon, 1955).

33. Kenneth M. Price, "Edition, Project, Database, Archive, Thematic Research Collection: What's in a Name?," *Digital Humanities Quarterly* 3, no. 3 (2009), par. 21.

34. For more on indices and knowledge creation, see Robin Valenza, "How Literature Becomes Knowledge: A Case Study," *ELH* 76, no. 1 (2009): 215–245.

35. James Mussell, "Too Much To Read: Toward a Bibliographical Utopia," Wolff Lecture at the Annual Meeting of the Research Society for Victorian Periodicals, Kansas City, MO, September 2016.

36. Price, "Edition, Project, Database, Archive," par. 19.

37. St. Clair, *The Reading Nation*, 186.

38. Charlotte Smith, *Ethelinde, or the Recluse of the Lake*, vol. 1 (London: Cadell, 1789), π2v, British Library copy, shelf mark Cup.403.i.8.

39. "Ethelinde, or Recluse of the Lake," *The Monthly Review* 2nd ser., 2 (June 1790): 162.

40. "Azemia; a descriptive and entertaining Novel," *The Monthly Review* 2nd ser., 24 (November 1797): 338. This novel's title page claims to be by J.A.M Jenks, now known to be a pseudonym used by William Beckford. The *Monthly* also prints a slightly different extended title for the work, calling it a "descripting and entertaining Novel," whereas the title page calls it "a descriptive and sentimental novel."

41. "The Man of Fortitude; or, Schedoni in England," *The Monthly Review* 2nd ser., 37 (January 1802): 28.

42. "An Essay on the Malignant Pestilential Fever," *The Monthly Review* 2nd ser., 36 (December 1801): 369–372.

43. Stephen M. Colclough has conducted this original research and outlines the extended reading practices of young Joseph Hunter in his "Procuring Books and Consuming Texts: The Reading Experience of a Sheffield Apprentice, 1798," *Book History* 3 (2000): 21–44. Hunter's reading practices have since been added to the online *Reading Experience Database*.

44. *UK RED*, record 10939, accessed February 3, 2017, http://www.open.ac.uk/Arts
/reading/UK/record_details.php?id=10939.

45. *UK RED*, record 10931, accessed February 3, 2025, http://www.open.ac.uk/Arts
/reading/UK/record_details.php?id=10931. Two years earlier, he recorded that he "got the
'Monthly Magazine' from Miss Haynes who takes it in," suggesting that Haynes is not
associated with the lending library (record 9875, accessed March 11, 2025, http://www
.open.ac.uk/Arts/reading/UK/record_details.php?id=9875).

46. *UK RED*, record 10855, accessed January 23, 2025, http://www.open.ac.uk/Arts
/reading/UK/record_details.php?id=10855.

47. Colclough, "Procuring Books," 26.

48. Colclough, "Procuring Books," 32.

49. Colclough, "Procuring Books," 35

50. Colclough, "Procuring Books," 35

51. Jerome McGann, "Database, Interface, and Archival Fever," *PMLA*, 122 no. 5
(2007): 1588–1592, 1590.

Chapter 2 · A Dialogue in Print

1. Regina Maria Roche, *The Vicar of Lansdowne; or, the Country Quarters. A Tale*,
vol. 1, 2 vols. (London: J. Johnson, 1789). Roche's maiden name was Dalton. This is the
only novel published with "Regina Maria Dalton" on the title page, so I refer to her by
the name she would have been best known by during her lifetime, her married name of
Roche. *The Women's Print History Project* also uses Roche for the author's name authority
file. "Roche I, Regina Maria," *The Women's Print History Project*, 2019, Person ID 518,
accessed July 9, 2025, https://womensprinthistoryproject.com/person/518.

2. *NRD*, https://bibsite.orgDetail/objects/218.

3. "The Vicar of Lansdowne; Or Country Quarters," *The Monthly Review* 2nd ser., 1
(February 1790): 222–223.

4. "The Vicar of Lansdowne; Or Country Quarters," 222.

5. For more details on how people read Review periodicals and the expected format
of novel reviews, see Chapter 1; Megan Peiser, "Reviews as Database: Reading the Review
Periodical in Eighteenth-Century England," *The Papers of the Bibliographical Society of
America* 111, no. 4 (November 14, 2017): 491–511; Megan Peiser, "William Lane and the
Minerva Press in the Review Periodical, 1790–1820," *Romantic Textualities: Literature and
Print Culture, 1780–1840* 23 (August 30, 2020): 124–148.

6. Roche, The Vicar of Lansdowne; or, the Country Quarters," 223.

7. Roche, *The Vicar of Lansdowne; or, the Country Quarters. A Tale*, 1:[iv].

8. Roche, 1:[v].

9. Roche, 1:[v].

10. Roche, 1:[v].

11. "The Vicar of Landsdowne [sic]; Or, Country Quarters. A Tale," *The Critical Review* 67 (June 1789): 475.

12. The "Minerva Era" is defined in Hannah Doherty Hudson, *Romantic Fiction and
Literary Excess in the Minerva Press Era*, Cambridge Studies in Romanticism (Cambridge:
Cambridge University Press, 2023).

13. Laura Runge, "Churls and Graybeards and Novels Written by a Lady: Gender in

Eighteenth-Century Book Reviews," *CW3 Journal (Corvey Women Writers 1796–1834 on the Web)* 1 (Summer 2004).

14. See specifically Hannah Doherty Hudson, "Gothic before Gothic: Minerva Press Reviews, Gender and the Evolution of Genre," in *Women's Authorship and the Early Gothic: Legacies and Innovations*, ed. Kathleen Hudson, Gothic Literary Studies (Cardiff: University of Wales Press, 2020), 43–64.

15. Jennie Batchelor, *The Lady's Magazine (1770–1830) and the Making of Literary History*, Edinburgh Critical Studies in Romanticism (Edinburgh: Edinburgh University Press, 2022), 78; Betty A. Schellenberg, *The Professionalization of Women Writers in Eighteenth-Century Britain*, 1 Reissue ed. (Cambridge: Cambridge University Press, 2005), 13.

16. Jennie Batchelor, "The Claims of Literature: Women Applicants to the Royal Literary Fund, 1790–1810," *Women's Writing*, no. 3 (2005): 509–512.

17. Pam Perkins, "Reviewing Femininity: Gender and Genre in the Late Eighteenth- and Early Nineteenth-Century Periodical Press," in *Women's Periodical Culture in Britain, 1690–1820s*, ed. Jennie Batchelor and Manushag N. Powell, vol. 1 (Edinburgh: Edinburgh University Press, 2018), 261.

18. Elizabeth Neiman, *Minervas Gothics: The Politics and Poetics of Romantic Exchange, 1780–1820* (Cardiff: University of Wales Press, 2019), 26.

19. Hudson, "Gothic before Gothic."

20. All data for this chapter, including a full list of novels it considers, can be found in the *NRD* file, available on BibSite.org: https://bibsite.org/Detail/objects/218.

21. Kandice Sharren, "Data Intimacy at Scale: Getting to Know the Women's Print History Project," Society for the History of Authorship, Reading, and Publishing, Amherst, MA, 2019.

22. Peter Garside, James Raven, and Rainer Schöwerling, *The English Novel 1770–1829: A Bibliographical Survey of Prose Fiction Published in the British Isles: Volume I, 1770–1799* (Oxford: Oxford University Press, 2000).

23. For more on policing readers and genre, see Frank Donoghue, *The Fame Machine: Book Reviewing and Eighteenth-Century Literary Careers* (Stanford, CA: Stanford University Press, 1996), 17. While the Reviews did employ a few women reviewers across this period, the overwhelming majority of them were men. For their identifications, see Benjamin Christie Nangle's *The Monthly review, first series, 1749–1789; indexes of contributors and articles* (Oxford: Clarendon, 1934); and *The Monthly Review, second series, 1790–1815; indexes of contributors and articles* (Oxford: Clarendon, 1955). For women reviewers of novels, see Megan Peiser, "Reviewing Women: Women Reviewers on Women Novelists," in *Women's Periodicals and Print Culture in Britain, 1690–1820s: The Long Eighteenth Century*, ed. Jennie Batchelor and Manushag N. Powell, ix, The Edinburgh History of Women's Periodical Culture in Britain (Edinburgh: Edinburgh University Press, 2018), 236–249.

24. Hudson, "Gothic before Gothic," 60.

25. Jon Rowland suggests that in fact for some authors, the preface itself might *be* the text. Jon Rowland, "Another Turn of the Screw: Prefaces in Swift, Marvell, and Genette," *Studies in Eighteenth-Century Culture* 21, no. 1 (1992): 129–148.

26. Joseph F. Bartolomeo, *A New Species of Criticism: Eighteenth-Century Discourse on the Novel* (Newark, NJ: University of Delaware Press, 1994), 90–97.

27. Gerard Genette, *Paratexts: Thresholds of Interpretation* (Cambridge: Cambridge

University Press, 1997), 2; Katharina Rennhak, "Paratexts and the Construction of Author Identities: The Preface as Threshold and Thresholds in the Preface," in *Mediating Identities in Eighteenth-Century England: Public Negotiations, Literary Discourses, Topography*, ed. Isabel Karremann and Anja Müller, xiv (Surrey, UK: Ashgate, 2011), 57–70.

28. Hudson, *Romantic Fiction and Literary Excess in the Minerva Press Era*, 35.

29. Of the 867 novels by female or anonymous authors in the *NRD*, 350 include prefatory paratext. These 350 make up this study. Many of these prefaces call themselves by other names as well—introduction, advertisement, apology, dedication, letter, note. While Gerard Genette outlines the differences in these specific genres, his identifiers were not shared among the readers or writers of the late eighteenth century. Despite varying titles, the prefatory paratexts to novels during this period all serve the same function. I have therefore included any text preceding the main work in this study as well as those with similar labels that were occasionally bound behind the main text body, as their label or content suggests they are a part of the period's prefatory tradition.

30. Anna Maria Porter, *Artless Tales*, ed. Shannon Goetze and Leslie Robertson (Edmonton, CA: Juvenilia, 2003), 4.

31. Goetze and Robertson's edition, the only modern edition of Porter's novel in print, also notes "Public" to be a reference to the Reviews and their criticism and the inclusion of her "youth and inexperience" to be responses to popular review criticisms of novels.

32. For more on the Reviews' criticism of grammar, see Carol Percy, "Periodical Reviews and the Rise of Prescriptivism: The Monthly (1749–1844) and Critical Review (1756–1817) in the Eighteenth Century," in *Current Issues in Late Modern English*, ed. Ingrid Tieken-Boon van Ostade and Wim van der Wurff (Bern: Peter Lang, 2009), 117–150.

33. Porter, *Artless Tales*, 4.

34. "Calaf; a Persian Tale," *The Critical Review* 2nd ser., 25 (January 1799): 118.

35. "Calaf, a Persian Tale," *The Monthly Review* 2nd ser., 27 (December 1798): 453–454.

36. "Adeline St. Julian; Or, the Midnight Hour; a Novel," *The Critical Review* 2nd ser., 29 (May 1800): 116.

37. For more on women writers and the celebration of juvenile geniuses, see Devoney Looser's "Age and Ageing" in *The Cambridge Companion to Women's Writing in the Romantic Period*, ed. Devoney Looser (Cambridge: Cambridge University Press, 2015), 169–182.

38. "Ellen, Countess of Castle-Howel; a Novel," *The Monthly Review* 2nd ser., 14 (May 1794): 75. The author, Anna Maria Bennett, was 48 at the time of its publication, but the Reviews likely did not know this.

39. Batchelor, *The Lady's Magazine (1770–1830) and the Making of Literary History*, 50.

40. "Artless Tales," *The Critical Review* 2nd ser., 9 (September 1793): 95. This review is not catalogued in the *NRD*, as it does not introduce itself in any way as a novel. The *Critical* reviews a new volume of Porter's *Artless Tales* in October 1795, under the Monthly Catalogue heading of "Novels," however, and cites this previous 1793 review, thereby marking (belatedly) the work as a novel in their eyes. "Artless Tales," *The Critical Review* 2nd ser., 15 (October 1795): 236. For more on the writing and reception of Porter's *Artless Tales*, see Devoney Looser, *Sister Novelists: The Trailblazing Porter Sisters, Who Paved the Way for Austen and the Brontës* (New York: Bloomsbury, 2022), 31–33.

41. "The Duchess of York, an English Story," *The Critical Review* 2nd ser., 3 (September 1791): 117.

42. For more on the formulaic nature of the reviews and their parallel to the novels they critique, see Siv Gøril Brandtzæg, "Aversion to Imitation: The Rise of Literary Hierarchies in Eighteenth-Century Novel Reviews," *Forum for Modern Language Studies* 51, no. 2 (March 27, 2015): 171–185.

43. "The Memoirs of Emma Courtney," *The Monthly Review* 2nd ser., 22 (April 1797): 443–449.

44. "The Lake of Killarney," *The Monthly Review* 2nd ser., 47 (June 1805): 205–206.

45. "Bungay Castle: a Novel," *The Critical Review* 2nd ser., 21 (October 1797): 234–235.

46. "The History of Netterville, a chance Pedestrian," *The Monthly Review* 2nd ser., 40 (February 1803): 208.

47. "Agnes de Courci, a domestic tale," *The Monthly Review* 2nd ser., 1 (February 1790): 216. The novel received some blowback in reaction to its Catholic characters' ideas. The *Monthly* here suggests that the authoress could not possibly have these ideas herself but rather places them in the mouth of a priest for argument's sake. This is quite a compliment to her skill in crafting character.

48. "Aretas, a novel," *The Critical Review* 4th ser., 4 (July 1813): 107.

49. Emma Parker, *Aretas, a novel*, vol. 1, 4 vols. (London: Crosby, 1813), ii.

50. Emma Parker, *Virginia; or, the Peace of Amiens, a Novel*, vol. 1, 4 vols. (London: Crosby, 1811), vi.

51. "Virginia; or, the Peace of Amiens, a Novel," *The Critical Review* 4th ser., 1 (January 1812): 110.

52. "The Loyalists; an historical novel," *The Critical Review* 4th ser., 2 (September 1812): 277–281.

53. "Letters from Mrs. Palmerstone to her Daughter; inculcating Morality by entertaining Narratives," *The Critical Review* 3rd ser., 1 (January 804): 118; "Adonia, a desultory Story," *The Monthly Review* 2nd ser., 35 (August 1801): 427–428.

54. "Ulric and Ilvina: the Scandinavian Tale," *The Critical Review* 2nd ser., 21 (October 1797): 230–232.

55. Sarah Green, *Romance Readers and Romance Writers*, ed. Christopher Goulding (Pickering & Chatto, 2010).

56. For more on Green's novel as gothic parody, see Mercy Cannon, "On the Edges of Gothic Parody: The Neglected Work of Mrs F. C. Patrick and Sarah Green," *Eighteenth-Century Fiction* 32, no. 4 (Summer 2020): 579–598.

57. April London, *The Cambridge Introduction to the Eighteenth-Century Novel* (Cambridge: Cambridge University Press, 2012), 154.

58. Laurence Sterne, *The Life and Opinions of Tristram Shandy, Gentleman*, ed. Melvyn New and Joan New, vol. 1–3, The Florida Edition of the Works of Laurence Sterne (Gainesville: University Press of Florida, 1978), 1:227–238.

59. Elizabeth Clark, *The Advertisement: Or, Twenty Years Ago: A Novel*, vol. 1 (London: Longman, Hurst, Rees, Orme and Brown and Barratt and Son, 1818), vii; Roche, *The Vicar of Lansdowne; or, the Country Quarters. A Tale*, 1:i.

60. Clark, *The Advertisement*, 1:vii.

61. "The Advertisement, or Twenty Years ago," *The Monthly Review* 2nd ser., 86 (May 1818): 103.

62. For the implications of this claim via novels and the "history of the production of knowledge," see Anne Stevens, "Tales of Other Times: A Survey of British Historical Fiction 1770–1812," *Cardiff Corvey: Reading the Romantic Text*, December 1, 2001, http://digitalscholarship.unlv.edu/english_fac_articles/23; Christine Georgulis, "'This Is a True Story': Fiction Disguised as Fact in the Prefaces of Late Seventeenth and Eighteenth-Century French and English Prose Works," *Dissertation Abstracts International* 50, no. 5 (November 1989): 1299A–1299A.

63. Elizabeth Meeke, *Something Odd!: A Novel*, vol. 1 (London: Printed at the Minerva Press for A. K. Newman, 1804), i.

64. "Something Odd: a Novel," *The Critical Review* 3rd ser., 3 (October 1804): 238.

65. On Meeke's identification, see S. Macdonald, "The Review of English Studies Prize Essay: Identifying Mrs Meeke, Another Burney Family Novelis," *The Review of English Studies* 64, no. 265 (June 1, 2013): 367–385; Frances Burney, *Evelina*, ed. Edward A. Bloom, new ed., Oxford World's Classics (Oxford: Oxford University Press, 2008).

66. Mrs. Purcell, *The Orientalist: Or, Electioneering in Ireland: A Tale*, vol. 1 (London: Printed for Baldwin, Cradock, and Joy, J. Thomson, William Gribbin and Samuel Archer, 1820), viii.

Chapter 3 · *The Rise and Fall of Charlotte Smith, Novelist*

1. This number considers only her "adult" fiction and translations.

2. Counting all reviews of women writers indexed in Ann R. Hawkins and Stephanie Eckroth, eds., *Romantic Women Writers Reviewed*, 9 vols. (London: Routledge, 2011).

3. Carrol L. Fry, *Charlotte Smith*, 1st ed. (New York: Twayne, 1996).

4. See Appendix A for a complete list of authors and titles included in Anna Laetitia Barbauld's *British Novelists* (1810) and Sir Walter Scott's *Ballantyne's British Novelists* (1821–1824).

5. See, for example, Kaley Kramer, "Like Nobody Else: Women and Independence in the Novels of Charlotte Smith and Mary Wollstonecraft," in *The Routledge Companion to Literature and Feminism*, ed. Rachel Carroll and Fiona Tolan (New York: Routledge, 2024), 29–41; Jerrold E. Hogle, "From the Gothic Castle to the Romantic Haunted House: Disbelief, Conversion, Aporia, Abjection," *European Romantic Review* 34, no. 2 (April 1, 2023): 133–149; Renee Buesking, "Charlotte Smith's Forms of Protest," *European Romantic Review* 32, no. 3 (June 1, 2021): 261–277.

6. Foundationally, this work includes Charlotte Smith, *The Poems of Charlotte Smith*, ed. Stuart Curran (New York: Oxford University Press, 1993); Stuart Curran, "Charlotte Smith and British Romanticism," *South Central Review* 11, no. 2 (1994): 66–78; Stuart Curran, "Charlotte Smith, Mary Wollstonecraft, and the Romance of Real Life," in *The History of British Women's Writing, 1750–1830*, vol. 5, ed. Jacqueline M. Labbe (New York: Palgrave Macmillan, 2010), 194–206; Jacqueline M. Labbe, *Charlotte Smith: Romanticism, Poetry and the Culture of Gender* (Manchester: Manchester University Press, 2003); Jacqueline Labbe, *Charlotte Smith in British Romanticism* (London: Pickering & Chatto, 2008).

7. Jacqueline M. Labbe, *Writing Romanticism: Charlotte Smith and William Wordsworth, 1784–1807* (New York: Palgrave Macmillan, 2011).

8. Pamela Clemit and Brad Scott, "Botanical Networking: Four Holograph Letters from Charlotte Smith to James Edward Smith," *Romanticism: The Journal of Romantic*

Culture and Criticism 26, no. 1 (April 4, 2020): 1–12; Melissa Bailes, "Linnaeus's Botanical Clocks: Chronobiological Mechanisms in the Scientific Poetry of Erasmus Darwin, Charlotte Smith, and Felicia Hemans," *Studies in Romanticism* 56, no. 2 (Summer 2017): 223–252; Lisa Vargo, "Locating the Common in Charlotte Smith's Ecocritical Writings for Children," in *Placing Charlotte Smith*, ed. Elizabeth A. Dolanis and Jacqueline M. Labbe (Bethlehem, PA: Lehigh University Press, 2020), 137–157.

9. Judith Phillips Stanton, *The Collected Letters of Charlotte Smith* (Bloomington: Indiana University Press, 2003).

10. Louise Duckling, "'Tell My Name to Distant Ages': The Literary Fate of Charlotte Smith," in *Charlotte Smith in British Romanticism*, ed. Jacqueline Labbe (London: Pickering & Chatto, 2008), 203–217.

11. Michael Gamer, "Subscriptions Reprinting: The Third and Fifth Elegiac Sonnets," in *Romanticism, Self-Canonization, and the Business of Poetry* (London: Cambridge University Press, 2017), 73–74.

12. Labbe, *Writing Romanticism*, 103–104.

13. Labbe, *Charlotte Smith*, 44.

14. For more on Richard Smith's will and Smith's financial situation, see Loraine Fletcher, *Charlotte Smith: A Critical Biography*, rev. ed. (Basingstoke: Palgrave Macmillan, 1998), 54–58.

15. Duckling, "'Tell My Name to Distant Ages.'"

16. See Chapter 2.

17. Fletcher, *Charlotte Smith*, 92.

18. Stephen C. Behrendt, "Charlotte Smith, Women Poets, and the Culture of Celebrity," in *Charlotte Smith in British Romanticism*, ed. Jacqueline Labbe (London: Pickering & Chatto, 2008), 189–202.

19. Gamer, "Subscriptions Reprinting," 74–75; "Manon L'Escaut: or the Fatal Attraction. A French Story," *The Monthly Review* 1st ser., 75 (October 1786): 316.

20. Stuart Curran, "Charlotte Smith: Intertextualities," in *Charlotte Smith in British Romanticism*, ed. Jacqueline Labbe (London: Routledge, 2008), 188.

21. Labbe, *Writing Romanticism*, 24.

22. For a detailed discussion on review placement and eighteenth-century reading practices, see Chapter 1 and Megan Peiser, "Reviews as Database: Reading the Review Periodical in Eighteenth-Century England," *The Papers of the Bibliographical Society of America* 111, no. 4 (November 14, 2017): 491–511.

23. "Emmeline; A Novel," *The Monthly Review* 2nd ser., 79 (September 1788): 242.

24. "Emmeline," *The Critical Review* no. 65 (June 1788): 530. Peter Garside, James Raven, and Rainer Schöwerling's bibliography inexplicably does not list the *Critical's* review of *Emmeline*, though it does list the *Monthly's*. See *The English Novel 1770–1829: A Bibliographical Survey of Prose Fiction Published in the British Isles: Volume I, 1770–1799* (Oxford: Oxford University Press, 2000), 448.

25. "Celestina" *Critical Review* 2nd ser., 3 (Nov 1791): 318–323.

26. Richard Brinsley Sheridan, *The Critic; or, A Tragedy Rehearsed. A Comedy in Three Acts as it is performed at the Theatre Royal in Drury Lane* (London: T. Becket, 1781), iii.

27. "The Young Philosopher," *The Critical Review* 2nd ser., 24 (September 1798): 77. In 1793 Frances Burney married French émigré Alexandre D'Arblay. The Reviews refer to her by her married name after this point.

28. Most others who had their first novel reviewed in the front section had, like Smith, published in other genres previously. For example, Elizabeth Inchbald's *A Simple Story* (1791) is reviewed by both Reviews in the front section, following her nearly ten-year career writing for the stage. Frances Burney (*Evelina* in the *Critical*) and Jane Austen (*Sense and Sensibility* in the *Critical*) are of the few who managed front-section reviews for their first novel with no previously published work.

29. While we know that reviewers were paid by the sheet for their reviews, this seems to be by the sheet of their criticism (not excerpt). For more on the reviewing practices and pay schemes of the Reviews, see Antonia Forster, "Review Journals and the Reading Public," in *The History of the Book in the West, Volume III: 1700–1800*, ed. Eleanor S. Shevlin and Alexis Weedon (Farnham, UK: Ashgate, 2010), 379–398.

30. See "Procedure for Compiling and Guide for Using the *Novels Reviewed Database, 1790–1820*," at Bibsite.org: https://bibsite.org/Detail/objects/218.

31. The 1800s novel with top page space, a translation of Kotzebue's *The Pastor's Daughter*, was possibly one of many novels that publisher Henry Colburn published simultaneously in English for his English and Foreign Circulating Library and in German on the continent, as he was wont to do. It does appear in an 1805 collected works of Kotzebue in German, so it is also possible that this novel had been circulating either in German or English before 1807, therefore gaining popularity: *Kleine Romane, Erzählungen, Anekdoten und Miscellen*, 2 vols. (Berlin: Paul Gotthelf Kummer, 1805).

32. In the entire *NRD* (January 1790 to December 1820), the author whose novels receive the most pages of review is unsurprisingly Sir Walter Scott (Table 3.3). His *The Monastery* (1820) receives the most attention: 22.5 pages—3.75 of excerpts and 18.75 pages of criticism. The 1810s also shows a surprising absence: Not a single novel by Jane Austen makes the chart.

33. Judith Davis Miller, "The Politics of Truth and Deception: Charlotte Smith and the French Revolution," in *Rebellious Hearts: British Women Writers and the French Revolution*, ed. Adriana Craciun, Kari E. Lokke, and Madelyn Gutwirth, SUNY Series in Feminist Criticism and Theory (Albany: State University of New York Press, 2001), 337–363; Amy Garnai, *Revolutionary Imaginings in the 1790s: Charlotte Smith, Mary Robinson, Elizabeth Inchbald* (New York: Palgrave Macmillan, 2009); Harriet Guest, "Charlotte Smith, Mary Robinson and the First Year of the War with France," in *The History of British Women's Writing, 1750–1830*, ed. Jacqueline M. Labbe (New York: Palgrave Macmillan, 2010), 207–230; Kari Lokke, "Charlotte Smith's Desmond: The Historical Novel as Social Protest," *Women's Writing* 16, no. 1 (May 2009): 60–77.

34. For more on reviews of Smith by contemporary radical Mary Wollstonecraft, see Curran, "Charlotte Smith, Mary Wollstonecraft, and the Romance of Real Life."

35. Stanton, *The Collected Letters of Charlotte Smith*, 88.

36. Fletcher, *Charlotte Smith*, 239–241.

37. "Old Manor House," *The Monthly Review* 2nd ser., 11 (June 1793): 153.

38. "Desmond," *The Monthly Review* 2nd ser., 9 (December 1792): 406.

39. See Chapter 1 for the ways page space made arguments to Review readers and the guide on Bibsite.org for how the *NRD* tracks page space in the periodicals: https://bibsite .org/Detail/objects/218.

40. "The Wanderings of Warwick," *The Monthly Review* 2nd ser., 14 (May 1794): 113.

41. "Letters of a Solitary Wanderer," *The Monthly Review* 2nd ser., 39 (December

1802): 428. Whether or not this work by Smith is or is not a novel is questionable. The *Orlando: Women's Writing in the British Isles* project classes it as a "Tale," noting that it is "somewhat in the manner of the *Canterbury Tales* by Harriet and Sophia Lee." The Reviews call this work a novel, which is why it is included in the *NRD*. Garside, Raven, and Schöwerling also include *Letters of a Solitary Wanderer* in their bibliography of prose fiction.

42. "The Old Manor House," *The Critical Review* 2nd ser., 8 (May 1793): 45.

43. "Montalbert," *The Critical Review* 2nd ser., 20 (August 1797): 469. Jane Austen's now-famous lament about the "Trash with which the press now groans" duplicates Review rhetoric. See Joseph F. Bartolomeo, *A New Species of Criticism: Eighteenth-Century Discourse on the Novel* (Newark, NJ: University of Delaware Press, 1994), 112–132.

44. *Ethelinde* (1789) included a dedication, but otherwise *Desmond* is the first to include a preface.

45. Sarah Zimmerman, "Charlotte Smith's Letters and the Practice of Self-Presentation," *The Princeton University Library Chronicle* 53, no. 1 (October 1, 1991): 60.

46. Charlotte Smith, *Desmond*, ed. Antje Blank and Janet Todd (Ontario: Broadview, 2001), 45.

47. Hannah Doherty Hudson, *Romantic Fiction and Literary Excess in the Minerva Press Era*, Cambridge Studies in Romanticism (Cambridge: Cambridge University Press, 2023), 60.

48. "Desmond," *The Monthly Review* 2nd ser., 9 (December 1792): 400.

49. "Desmond," *The Critical Review* 2nd ser., 6 (September 1792): 100.

50. Hannah Doherty Hudson, "Gothic before Gothic: Minerva Press Reviews, Gender and the Evolution of Genre," in *Women's Authorship and the Early Gothic: Legacies and Innovations*, ed. Kathleen Hudson, Gothic Literary Studies (Cardiff: University of Wales Press, 2020), 53.

51. Charlotte Smith, *The Banished Man*, 4 vols. (London: T. Cadell Jr. and Davies, 1794), 1:viii.

52. "The Banished Man," *The Critical Review* 2nd ser., 32 (March 1795): 275.

53. *Banished Man*, 1:v–vi.

54. "The Banished Man," *The Monthly Review* 2nd ser., 16 (February 1795): 133.

55. Jacqueline M. Labbe, "Selling One's Sorrows: Charlotte Smith, Mary Robinson, and the Marketing of Poetry," *The Wordsworth Circle* 25, no. 2 (Spring 1994): 68–71.

56. Charlotte Smith, *Marchmont; a Novel*, 4 vols. (London: Sampson Low, 1796), 1:vi.

57. Smith, *Marchmont*.

58. "Marchmont," *The Monthly Review* 2nd ser., 22 (April 1797): 468.

59. See Chapter 1 for reviewing traditions.

60. "Emmeline; or, the Orphan of the Castle," *The Critical Review* 65 (June 1788): 531.

61. Hudson, "Gothic before Gothic," 57. For more on professional women writers of this era, see George Justice, *The Manufacturers of Literature: Writing and the Literary Marketplace in Eighteenth-Century England* (Newark, DE: University of Delaware Press, 2002); Betty A. Schellenberg, "From Propensity to Profession: Female Authorship and the Early Career of Frances Burney," *Eighteenth-Century Fiction* 14, no. 3–4 (July 4, 2002): 345–370; Betty A. Schellenberg, *The Professionalization of Women Writers in Eighteenth-Century Britain*, reissue ed. (Cambridge: Cambridge University Press, 2005).

62. Clifford Siskin, *The Work of Writing: Literature and Social Change in Britain, 1700–1830* (Baltimore, MD: Johns Hopkins University Press, 1999), 218.

63. Jennie Batchelor, *The Lady's Magazine (1770–1830) and the Making of Literary History*, Edinburgh Critical Studies in Romanticism (Edinburgh: Edinburgh University Press, 2022), 210–222.

64. Michael Gamer, "A Select Collection: Barbauld, Scott, and the Rise of the (Reprinted) Novel," in *Recognizing the Romantic Novel: New Histories of British Fiction, 1780–1830*, ed. Jillian Heydt-Stevenson and Charlotte Sussman (Liverpool: Liverpool University Press, 2008), 156–157.

65. For more on the history, tradition, and proliferation of newspaper and periodical reprints of texts, see Ryan Cordell and David Smith, *Viral Texts: Mapping Networks of Reprinting in 19th-Century Newspapers and Magazines*, The Viral Texts Project (2024), accessed July 10, 2025, http://viraltexts.org.

66. Gamer, "A Select Collection," 179.

67. From an announcement for the series in *The Athenaeum: a magazine of literary and miscellaneous information*, no. 2 (November 1807): 513. The announcement includes Smith in the list of authors included: "Will include the most admired Novels of Richardson, Fielding, Mrs. Brookes, Smollett, Mackenzie, Goldsmith, Walpole, Dr. Moore, Johnson, C. Smith, Mrs. Radcliffe, Mrs. Inchbald, Mrs. D'Arblay, and other popular writers."

68. See Appendix A for a list of works included in Barbauld's *British Novelists*.

69. See Appendix A. Claudia Johnson also doubts that copyright issues influenced the exclusion of authors from Barbauld's collection and that the length of novels might have had more of an influence. Novels included were all about the same length (3–4 volumes in their original publication), which would only exclude Smith's *Ethelinde* (5 vols.) from her earlier successful works. Claudia L. Johnson, "'Let Me Make the Novels of a Country': Barbauld's The British Novelists (1810/1820)," *Novel: A Forum on Fiction* 34, no. 2 (Spring 2001): 167.

70. Charlotte Smith receives eight pages of prefatory material from Barbauld, the same number as Radcliffe. Gamer makes a point to note how high Burney is on this list (fifth after Richardson, Fielding, Smollett, Goldsmith), but Smith is in the ranks of many other eight-page prefacers: Defoe, Johnson, and Radcliffe. And so Burney, Radcliffe, and Smith still manage to make up a trio in Barbauld's collection.

71. Anna Laetitia Barbauld, *The British Novelists*, 50 vols. (London: Rivington, 1810): 36:vii–viii.

72. "Old Manor House," *Monthly*, 153.

73. "Old Manor House," *Critical*, 52–53.

74. Barbauld, 36:vi–vii.

75. Johnson, "'Let Me Make the Novels of a Country,'" 174.

76. See Appendix A for novels included in Ballantyne's.

77. Scott also places Defoe in this collection instead of in *BNL*.

78. *Public Characters of 1800–1801* (London: R. Phillips, 1801), 42–64. For how the *Public Characters* piece represented Smith as a poet, see Duckling, "'Tell My Name to Distant Ages,'" 205.

79. John Hepburn Millar, *The Mid-Eighteenth Century* (New York: W. Blackwood and sons, 1902), 143.

80. Duckling, "'Tell My Name to Distant Ages,'" 205.

81. Samuel Griswold Goodrich, *The Token and Atlantic Souvenir: A Christmas and New Year's Present* (Boston, MA: Charles Bowen, 1836), 133.

82. Scott took up the seat in 1827 after the confirmed outing of his authorship (already popular public knowledge) of the *Waverley* series.

83. Julia Kavanagh, *English Women of Letters: Biographical Sketches*, vol. 1 (Leipzig: Bernhard Tauchnitz, 1862), 187–188.

84. James R. Foster, "Charlotte Smith, Pre-Romantic Novelist," *PMLA: Publications of the Modern Language Association of America* 43, no. 2 (1928): 473.

85. Foster, "Charlotte Smith," 475.

86. Stuart Curran, "The Records of Woman's Romanticism," *Women's Writing*, April 3, 2015, 268.

Chapter 4 · A Study in 55 Novels

1. Althea Fanshawe, *Easter Holidays, or Domestic Conversations, Designed for the Instruction, and It Is Hoped for the Amusement of Young People* (Bath, 1797), unsigned A2, Eighteenth-Century Collections Online.

2. Charlotte Turner Smith, *Rural Walks: In Dialogues. Intended for the Use of Young Persons. By Charlotte Smith. In Two Volumes. . . .*, vol. 1 (London: printed for T. Cadell jun. and W. Davies, successors to Mr. Cadell, in the Strand, 1795), iii, Eighteenth-Century Collections Online.

3. Fanshawe, *Easter Holidays.*

4. See Table 2.1 from Chapter 2 "A Dialogue in Print: Reviews and Novel Prefaces."

5. Peter Garside, James Raven, and Rainer Schöwerling, *The English Novel 1770–1829: A Bibliographical Survey of Prose Fiction Published in the British Isles: Volumes I and II* (Oxford: Oxford University Press, 2000).

6. Andrew Block, *The English Novel, 1740–1850 ; a Catalogue Including Prose Romances, Short Stories, and Translations of Foreign Fiction* (London: Dawsons of Pall Mall, 1962).

7. "Tales from Shakespeare," *The Critical Review* 3rd ser., 11 (May 1807): 98; "A Tale of Rosamund Gray and old Blind Margaret," *The Critical Review* 2nd ser., 25 (April 1799): 472–473.

8. *"Felissa," The Critical Review* 3rd ser., 11 (April 1811): 443.

9. Jacqueline Belanger et al., "The English Novel, 1800–1829: Update 4 (June 2003–August 2004)," *Romantic Textualities* 12 (Summer 2004): 83–116. It is unclear why the *Monthly's* original review of this work was either missed or insufficient for the editors' earliest consideration of *Paternal Love* as a novel.

10. M. O. Grenby, *The Child Reader, 1700–1840* (Cambridge: Cambridge University Press, 2011).

11. Jenny Mander notes that the 1790s and early 1800s were about "15 percent of the market for new fiction" in "Foreign Imports," in *English and British Fiction 1750–1820*, ed. Peter Garside and Karen O'Brien, vol. 2, The Oxford History of the Novel in English (Oxford: Oxford University Press, 2015), 589–612.

12. *The Story of Al-Raoui, a Tale from the Arabic* (1799) is indeed taken from a manuscript—but from one written in French in the style of a Persian tale by William Beckford, which here his friend Samuel Henry publishes in English without the author's permission. *Henrietta, Princess Royal of England. An Historical Novel* (1796) comes from the manuscript dictated to Madame de La Fayette, which later belonged to the Fanshawe

family. Either the aforementioned Althea Fanshaw from this chapter or her mother transcribed this manuscript, from which this edition was likely made.

13. The three works are *Henrietta, Princess Royal of England. An Historical Novel* (1796); *The Life and Extraordinary Adventures of James Molesworth Hobart, alias Henry Griffin, alias Lord Massey, the New-Market Duke of Ormond, &c. involving a number of well-known Characters: together with a short Sketch of the early part of the Life of Dr. Torquid* by John Collard (1794); and *Memoirs of a Picture, Containing the Adventures of many conspicuous Characters, connected with the Arts, and including a genuine Biographical Sketch of the late Mr. George Morland* by William Collins (1805).

14. The data about these three works included in this chapter's dataset is a guess based on review information. All errors about them are my own.

15. G. Thomas Tanselle, "Textual Study and Literary Judgment," *The Papers of the Bibliographical Society of America* 65, no. 2 (1971): 109–122.

16. Garside, Raven, and Schöwerling, *The English Novel 1770–1829*, 3.

17. Garside, Raven, and Schöwerling, *The English Novel 1770–1829*, 3.

18. Garside, Raven, and Schöwerling, *The English Novel 1770–1829*, 4. See the "Procedure for Compiling and Guide for Using the *Novels Reviewed Database, 1790–1820*" for outline of how the *NRD* was created and how it aligns with and differs from the Garside and Raven bibliography, https://bibsite.org/Detail/objects/218.

19. Peter Garside, James Raven, and Rainer Schöwerling, *The English Novel 1770–1829: A Bibliographical Survey of Prose Fiction Published in the British Isles: Volume II, 1800–1829* (Oxford: Oxford University Press, 2000), 35.

20. Lauren Klein, "Distant Reading After Moretti," paper presented at the Modern Language Association MLA annual convention, New York City, NY, January 2018. https://lklein.com/digital-humanities/distant-reading-after-moretti/.

21. Margaret J. M. Ezell, *Writing Women's Literary History* (Baltimore, MD: Johns Hopkins University Press, 1996).

22. Nicole C. Woitowich, Annaliese Beery, and Teresa Woodruff, "A 10-Year Follow-up Study of Sex Inclusion in the Biological Sciences," ed. Cassidy Sugimoto et al., *eLife* 9 (June 9, 2020).

23. Marisa J. Fuentes, *Dispossessed Lives: Enslaved Women, Violence, and the Archive* (Philadelphia: University of Pennsylvania Press, 2016).

24. Imtiaz Habib, *Black Lives in the English Archives, 1500–1677: Imprints of the Invisible*, 1st ed. (Aldershot, UK: Routledge, 2007), 9.

25. It is my hope that the dual publication of this book alongside digital access to the *NRD* will enable its data to be a more helpful tool for those who will use it and that it will be better able to answer for itself in my absence.

26. Many thanks to Deirdre Marculescu, historian and volunteer at Valence House Library and expert on the Fanshawe Family, for sharing her knowledge about Althea and her family's situation. Her research and transcriptions of Fanshawe's diary can be found in her *From My Window: The Diary of Althea Fanshawe* (Dagenham, UK: Valence House Publications, 2025).

27. My many thanks to Jason Farr for assisting in this research inquiry.

28. Smith, *Rural Walks*, 1:iv.

29. "Rural Walks," *The Monthly Review* 2nd ser.,17 (July 1795): 349–350. It should be noted that **no** novels are reviewed in this issue.

30. This is also consistent with the *Critical's* treatment of Smith's novels at the time. See Chapter 3, but also not calling it a "novel" is why this review is not included in the *NRD*.

31. Smith, *Rural Walks*, 1:iv.

32. "Easter Holidays," *The Monthly Review* 2nd ser., 26 (June 1798): 222.

33. "Easter Holidays," *The Critical Review* 2nd ser., 27 (October 1799): 228.

34. Katherine Bode, *A World of Fiction: Digital Collections and the Future of Literary History*, Digital Humanities (Ann Arbor: University of Michigan Press, Australian National University, 2018), 6.

35. This guide deposited on Bibsite.org along with the *NRD*: https://bibsite.org /Detail/objects/218.

36. M. O. Grenby, "Children's Literature, the Home, and the Debate on Public versus Private Education, c. 1760–1845," in *Home Education in Historical Perspective: Domestic Pedagogies in England and Wales, 1750–1900*, ed. Christina De Bellaigue (New York: Routledge, 2016), 46.

37. Grenby, "Children's Literature," 45.

38. Grenby, *The Child Reader, 1700–1840*, 112.

39. Grenby, *The Child Reader, 1700–1840*, 115.

40. Ann Harrison Fanshawe and H. C. (Herbert Charles) Fanshawe, *The Memoirs of Ann, Lady Fanshawe, Wife of the Right Honble Sir Richard Fanshawe, Bart., 1600–72* (London: John Lane, 1907), 222.

41. Wellcome Library MS. 7113. Lady Fanshawe's recipe book is now part of the *Early Modern Recipes Online Collective* initiatives: https://emroc.hypotheses.org/

42. Althea Fanshawe, "Will of Althea Fanshawe, Spinster of Walcot, Somerset," April 28, 1824, The National Archives Kew.

43. H. C. (Herbert Charles) Fanshawe, *The History of the Fanshawe Family* (Newcastle-upon-Tyne: A. Reid, 1927), 273–274.

44. Althea Fanshawe, *Thoughts on Affectation: Addressed Chiefly to Young People* (Bath: Richard Cruttwell, 1805), 296.

45. The highest number of "fits" recorded was 58 in 1815, and the most "attacks" was 327 in 1816.

46. Althea Fanshawe, "Althea Fanshawe's Diary 1805–1824 (Uncatalogued)," n.d., 112, ACQ2016/015, London Borough of Barking and Dagenham, Archives, Valence House.

47. Travis Chi Wing Lau, "Chronic and Invisible: The Future of Romantic Disability Studies," *Keats-Shelley Journal* 68 (2019): 137.

48. Fanshawe, "Althea Fanshawe's Diary 1805–1824 (Uncatalogued)," 46, 62, 82.

49. Fanshawe, "Althea Fanshawe's Diary 1805–1824 (Uncatalogued)," 90–91.

50. Margaret Price, "The Bodymind Problem and the Possibilities of Pain," *Hypatia* 30, no. 1 (2015): 268–284.

51. Alison Kafer, *Feminist, Queer, Crip* (Bloomington: Indiana University Press, 2013), 27.

52. Fanshawe, *Thoughts on Affectation*, 259.

53. Fanshawe, *Thoughts on Affectation*, 264.

54. My thanks to Richard A. Roberts for his help deciphering and understanding the probate wills of Althea Fanshawe the elder and younger. Althea Fanshawe, "Will of

Althea Fanshawe, Widow of Shiplake, Oxfordshire," January 31, 1805, The National Archives Kew; Fanshawe, "Will of Althea Fanshawe, Spinster of Walcot, Somerset."

55. H. C. Fanshawe's 1907 edition of *The Memoirs of Ann, Lady Fanshawe* records multiple instances of Fanshawe women bequeathing monies, properties, and possessions to female family members.

56. Ethelinda Margaretta Potts, *Moonshine* (London: Longman, Hurst, Rees, Orme and Brown, 1814), vi, HathiTrust.

57. "Moonshine," *The Monthly Review* 2nd ser., 75 (November 1814): 328.

58. Potts, *Moonshine*, 1814 vol I, 12.

59. Franco Moretti, "Style, Inc. Reflections on Seven Thousand Titles (British Novels, 1740–1850) on JSTOR," *Critical Inquiry* 36, no. 1 (Autumn 2009): 146–147.

60. For a more extensive study on genre labels across the eighteenth century, see Leah Orr, "Genre Labels on the Title Pages of English Fiction, 1660–1800," *Philological Quarterly* 90, no. 1 (Winter 2011): 67–95.

61. Antonia Forster, *Index to Book Reviews in England, 1749–1774* (Carbondale: Southern Illinois University Press, 1990), 16n32.

62. Throughout, I largely refer to Ethelinda Margaretta Potts by her first name, using the method that Judith Phillips Stanton adopts for Charlotte Smith in *The Collected Letters of Charlotte Smith* (2003). Because she abandoned her husband (and thereby possibly his name) and never put that name to her published works, I feel that this is a small way that I can return Ethelinda's personal and authorial agency to her. I acknowledge that these gender pronouns are assumed. I generally use "Potts" to refer to Ethelinda's estranged husband, Cuthbert Potts.

63. J. R. de J. Jackson, "Jackson Bibliography of Romantic Poetry," Jackson Bibliography of Romantic Poetry, accessed July 13, 2025, https://jacksonbibliography.library .utoronto.ca/.

64. Edward Hasted, "Parishes: Bexley," in *The History and Topographical Survey of the County of Kent*, vol. 2, British History Online (Canterbury, 1797), 162–183.

65. Ethelinda Thorpe was Potts's second wife; his first, Mary Dorothy Rich, died in 1780. Joseph Jackson Howard, "Potts, Formerly of Berwick-on-Tweed Co. Northumberland," in *Visitation of England and Wales*, ed. Frederick Arthur Crisp, vol. 14 (Priv. printed, 1906), 78–80.

66. John Thorpe et al., *Registrum Roffense, or, A collection of antient records, charters, and instruments of divers kinds : necessary for illustrating the ecclesiastical history and antiquities of the diocese and cathedral church of Rochester* (London: Printed for the editor, by W. and J. Richardson and sold by T. Longman . . . R. Dodsley . . . J. Murray . . . [and 3 others], 1769).

67. "Fifty Pounds Reward," *The Sun* no. 1556 (June 9, 1796): 1.

68. "Fifty Pounds Reward," *The Sun* no. 1158 (June 11, 1796): 1; Cuthbert Potts, *Fifty pounds reward! Whereas, Ethelinda Margaretta Potts, the wife of Cuthbert Potts, of Pall-Mall, . . . hath absented herself from her said husband, and cruelly abandoned her three infant children: . . .* (London: n.p., 1796).

69. Great Britain Court of Chancery, "Meggison v. Moore," in *Reports of Cases Argued and Determined in the High Court of Chancery: From the Year 1789 to 1817*, vol. 2 (London: S. Sweet and Stevens and Sons, 1827), 630–633.

70. Potts, *Moonshine*, [iii]; vii.

71. Potts, *Moonshine*, [1]; 12.

72. Potts, *Moonshine*, 90.

73. Potts, *Moonshine*, 91.

74. Potts, *Moonshine*, 91, 92.

75. A 2018 bookseller's description suggests that the book is an attempt to contact her estranged family, but the occasional poems here imply that she did in fact have contact with her children in the 1790s and early 1800s. Pickering & Chatto Bulletin 56, February 2018, http://pickering-chatto.com/PC/Catalogues_and_Lists_files/Bull56.pdf. For more on self-published works in the late eighteenth and early nineteenth centuries, see Emily Spunaugle, "'Printed for the Benefit': British Women's Benevolent Publications in the Long Eighteenth Century" (PhD diss., Wayne State University, 2024).

76. Ethelinda Margaretta Thorpe Potts, *Moonshine: Containing Sketches in England and Wales* (London: Davison, Simmons, 1832).

77. The table of contents in the 1832, 1833, and single-volume 1835 printings tell their volume number.

78. Ethelinda Margaretta Potts, *Moonshine: Containing Unconnected Trifles and Appendix*, vol. 3 (London: William Wilockson, 1835), 365.

79. Potts, *Moonshine: Containing Unconnected Trifles and Appendix*, 1835, 3:283–289.

80. Susan S. Lanser, *The Sexuality of History* (Chicago: University of Chicago Press, 2014), 7. From Lanser, I take up the term "Sapphic" to identify the relationship between Ethelinda and Sally Langford, noting that "lesbian" as a word and contexts by modern definition did not exist in the eighteenth century. "Sapphic" centers the intimacy of these women's relationship while allowing for ambiguity and the uncertainty of our knowledge or understanding about the various facets of their connection.

81. Lanser, *The Sexuality of History*, 6.

82. Ann Sarah Langford Potts. Birth: 1822, Buried: September 2, 1823, St. Keyne Churchyard, Kenwyn, Cornwall, UK. *National Burial Index for England and Wales*. Ancestry.com. My thanks to Chelsea Phillips and Emily Spunaugle for help with this query.

83. Potts, *Moonshine*, 89.

84. Benjamin Langford Forster Potts. Baptized: August 18, 1839, St. James's Picadilly, London, UK. *England and Wales, Birth Registration Index, 1837–2008*. Ancestry.com.

85. Potts, *Moonshine: Containing Sketches in England and Wales*, 65. Thanks to Kate Ozment and Shannon Supple for helping me access this volume.

86. Potts, *Moonshine: Containing Unconnected Trifles and Appendix*, 3:277.

87. Potts, *Moonshine: Containing Unconnected Trifles and Appendix*, 3:353.

88. Potts, *Moonshine: Containing Unconnected Trifles and Appendix*, 3:257–259. The footnote to "queens of May" reads: "1832 Now in the 40th year."

89. Bonnie Ruberg, Jason Boyd, and James Howe, "Toward a Queer Digital Humanities," in *Bodies of Information: Intersectonal Feminism and Digital Humanities*, Debates in Digital Humanities (Minneapolis: University of Minnesota, 2018).

90. Ruberg, Boyd, and Howe, "Toward a Queer Digital Humanities."

91. Potts, *Moonshine: Containing Sketches in England and Wales*, 34.

92. Potts, *Moonshine*, 167.

93. Ruberg, Boyd, and Howe, "Toward a Queer Digital Humanities."

94. Kirstyn Leuner, "Restoring Authority for Women Writers: Name Authority Records as Digital Recovery Scholarship," *Huntington Library Quarterly* 84, no. 1 (2021): 20.

95. Laura Mandell, "Gender and Cultural Analytics: Finding or Making Stereotypes?," in *Debates in the Digital Humanities 2019*, ed. Matthew K. Gold and Lauren F. Klein (Minneapolis: University of Minnesota Press, 2019), 3–26.

Postscript

1. Margaret J. M. Ezell, "Invisible Women, 1983–2021," *Huntington Library Quarterly* 84, no. 1 (2021): 9.

2. Ezell, "Invisible Women," 9.

3. Ezell, "Invisible Women," 9.

4. Ezell, "Invisible Women"; Michelle Levy and Betty A. Schellenberg, "Hiding in Plain Sight," *Huntington Library Quarterly* 84, no. 1 (2021): 205–212.

5. Ezell, "Invisible Women," 12.